(above) A two-mast sailboat called a schooner heels (leans over) to port in the wind; it is kept from rolling over too far by the design of the keel—this is like an upside down shark's fin or blade, sticking down from the bottom of the hull

(previous page) A great white shark chases some bait, Guadalupe, Caribbean

Discover.
Learn.
Live.

Lessons
for
Life

SEA SCHOOL

Mark Philpott

WHITE STAR LINE

Ready for a voyage?

I've got to be honest... I have never been one of those people who is eager to go swimming in the sea. I drink far too much of it. However, I have always loved being by the seaside. The thunderous sound of the crashing waves, the spray on your face, and the smell of salty air is good for the soul.

My grandparents lived at Hastings on the South Coast of England where there was still a thriving fishing industry, and most school holidays we would stay with them; it was a free vacation! My childhood is filled with memories like watching the lifeboat launching, the smell of

POST CARD freshly-caught fish, and the wailing of seagulls.

In the 1980s, at a time when we didn't have any money for expensive holidays, I had the luxury of skimming the surf in my cousin's speedboat as we went on holiday together every year. My cousin was a bit of a lad and we got into a few sticky situations.

These experiences have stayed with me, and I hope that this book about all things 'marine' gives you a taste for the sea also. I pray that you will learn about the One who is deeper than the ocean and more powerful than any violent storm.

Mark Philpott, 2023

Me

Memories of Hastings in the 1970s

Speedboat summers, early 1980s

Watching the tide cover the causeway to Lindisfarne (Holy Island), 2011

Seal and seabird-spotting boat trip to the Farne Islands (home of Grace Darling), with my darling Grace, 2011

Never too old for dress-up; the RNLI Henry Blogg Museum, Cromer, 2018

Mackerel fishing, Cornwall, 2022

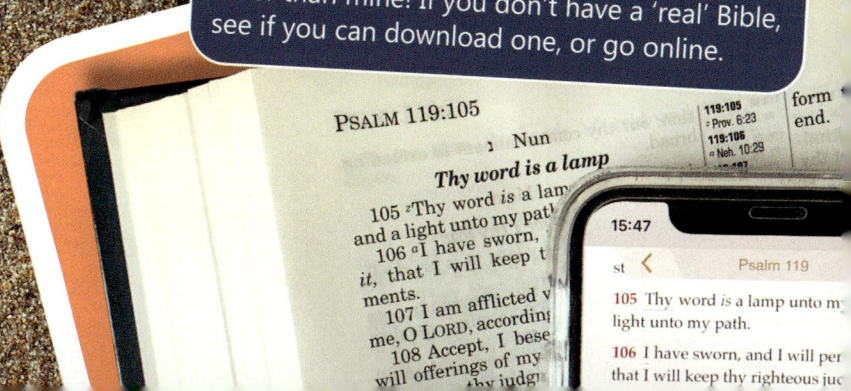

Before you start . . . get a Bible

As you read this book, look up the Bible quotes given in the blue boxes. God's words are much wiser than mine! If you don't have a 'real' Bible, see if you can download one, or go online.

PSALM 119:105

Nun

Thy word is a lamp

105 *Thy word is a lamp* and a light unto my path.

106 *I have sworn, it, that I will keep thy judg- ments.

107 I am afflicted me, O LORD, according

108 Accept, I bese will offerings of my will judg

119:105
Prov. 6:23
119:106
Neh. 10:29

form end.

15:47

Psalm 119

105 Thy word is a lamp unto my light unto my path.

106 I have sworn, and I will per that I will keep thy righteous jud

A scuba diver approaches the screw (propellor) of a shipwreck

Our Blue Planet 8

The Salty Sea 10

Tides 12

Ocean Currents 14

Oil and Gas Rigs 16

Fishing 18

Scuba Diving. 22

Sharks. 24

Deep Sea Creatures 26

Sea Monsters 28

Noah's Ark. 32

Ship Design. 34

Anchors 36

Storms at Sea. 38

Shipwrecks 42

The Titanic. 46

Life Preservers 48

Rescue at Sea. 50

Lighthouses. 56

Pirates. 60

The Slave Trade 62

Mercy Ships 64

Ports and Harbours 68

Beach Holiday 70

Lifeguards 72

Glossary 74

OUR BLUE PLANET

The ONLY place with liquid water

Gentle rainfall on the land—rain is vital for plants and animals

The Water of Life

Earth is the only known planet which has liquid water. Without it, there could be no life. When God made the world, it was covered with water; He knew what He was doing! Thankfully He divided the water from the land, so we would have somewhere to live. Water still covers over two-thirds of the Earth's surface. There is enough sea water to fill Wembley Stadium 145 times for each man, woman and child on Earth! When people ask where all the water went from Noah's Flood, the answer is that it is still in the sea. There is enough to cover a smooth Earth to a depth of about 2.7 km / 1.7 miles. Our weather and climate is largely dictated by the sun heating the oceans. Warmed water evaporates and the changes in air temperature cause a pressure difference, making the wind, which carries this moist air, forming clouds. The water falls as rain, before returning to the ocean in rivers. This is the water cycle, without which life on land would be impossible.

LEARNING POINT

The water cycle was described in the Bible (Ecclesiastes 1:7) centuries before scientists even understood it. There are several Bible portions which mention aspects of the water cycle—see Job 36:27-29 about evaporation of water to form clouds which drop as rain. The Bible can be trusted to speak accurately on all topics, not like scientists whose views can change over time.

Without water, life cannot continue. We can only go a few days without water or we will die. If there is no rain, plants would not grow, and animals and people would have no food. Why is there liquid water nowhere else in the known universe? If the universe was just an accident caused by a 'Big Bang', we would expect water elsewhere. But no. God made the Earth BEFORE He made the planets, sun and stars. Our planet is special. The whole universe exists because God has planned to make Man here, and to give eternal life to as many as He has purposed, by sending His Son Jesus on a rescue mission planned before He made the world.

THE BIBLE SAYS . . .
Jesus is the 'Lamb slain from [before] the foundation of the world.' (Revelation 13:8-9)
See 2 Timothy 1:9, 1 Peter 1:20

The Earth seen from space; a photo taken during the Apollo 17 mission by NASA

THE SALTY SEA

A pointer to the accuracy of Bible history

Not for you or me to drink

If you have swum in the sea you will know that sea water is very salty. It is thought that before Noah's Flood, the sea wasn't as salty as it is now; the effect of volcanoes during and after the Flood have contributed to the sea becoming more salty. Also groundwater has dissolved minerals and carried them by rivers into the sea, increasing its salinity. In fact, the seas are getting more salty every year. At the current rate of increase, the Earth <u>cannot</u> be billions of years old.

We must not drink sea water, because it is too salty for our bodies to cope with. Submarines, which may have to remain underwater for months, cannot take on board fresh supplies. They would run out of drinking water if they didn't have equipment for removing the salt from seawater. They do this by boiling the seawater and collecting the steam, which is then cooled, leaving the salt behind. Other technology can also be used to provide fresh drinking water on land, in desalination plants. They work on the principle of *reverse osmosis*, where water is forced at high pressure through a membrane (layer) designed to allow water molecules to pass through it, but not salt. These plants are expensive to run though, as they require a lot of energy.

LEARNING POINT

Sea creatures are designed or adapted to cope with high levels of salt in the water. Fish, for example, get rid of excess salt through their kidneys and gills. Although drinking a lot of seawater would quickly kill you or me, salt itself is essential for our bodies in the right amounts. In the ancient world, where there were no freezers or refrigerators, salt was very valuable because it is an excellent preservative; salting is still used today to keep fish and meat from spoiling. It also enhances the flavour of food.

We are all born sinners and, as a result, life can be a miserable experience because by nature we want to be selfish and not care for others. But when someone is born again and follows Jesus, they become a good influence in the world, helping and doing good. (Christians still fail sometimes!) They are like salt (Matthew 5:13), slowing the decay in society. They are also preserving nations from God's just punishment; see what God says in Genesis 18:32 to Abraham, about his intention to delay destroying Sodom, because Abraham's nephew Lot was there.

THE BIBLE SAYS . . .
God said, 'I will not destroy [Sodom] for ten's sake.' (Genesis 18:32)

See how all 276 people on board a ship in a violent storm were spared being drowned for the Apostle Paul's sake. (Acts 27:24)

(above) Submarines are able to extract drinking water from salty seawater by distillation

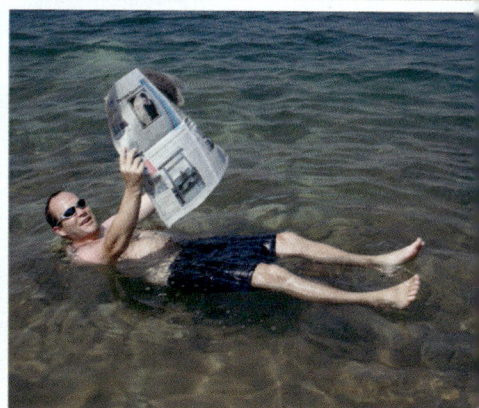

(above right x2) The Dead Sea, one of the saltiest bodies of water in the world; salt makes the water dense, so you can float more easily

(below) A desalination plant, California, USA

TIDES
The daily rise and fall of the sea

Time and tide wait for no man

Although we may not realise it, the Earth and everything on it are drawn to the moon. Wherever the moon is, seawater is attracted to it by gravity. This attraction raises the sea level, causing a *high tide* twice a day. In between, the water drops causing a *low tide*. It may seem unbelievable, but the tide is also affected by the sun, which is 93 million miles / 150 million km away. When the Earth, moon and sun all line up, it causes an extra surge called a 'spring tide'.

The height difference between high and low tides—the 'tidal range'—varies in different places depending on the shape of the sea bed and the coastline. The largest tidal range is Fundy Bay in Canada (53 ft. / 16.3m) where 115 billion tonnes of water flow in and out of the bay twice a day.

LEARNING POINT

As the tides are determined primarily by the movement of the Earth, moon and sun, which no man can control or influence, they are very predictable. Tide tables are published so that seafarers can make appropriate plans, such as the timing of when to launch a boat on a slipway. No-one can delay or stop the tide. There is a famous story of King Canute of England (990-1035AD) who sat in his chair on the seashore when the tide was coming in, commanding the water not to rise onto his land. But of course, he got wet! He is supposed to have then said, "Let all the world know that the power of kings is empty and worthless, and there is no king worthy of the name save Him by whose will Heaven, Earth and the sea obey eternal laws".

(above and left) St Ives harbour in Cornwall at high tide and at low tide

(below, left and right) Perch Rock lighthouse on the River Mersey at high tide (left), and at low tide (right)—the dotted white line indicates the high tide water line

(opposite page) The Bristol Channel between England and Wales has the 2nd highest tidal range in the world at 15m / 50 ft. The tide comes in rapidly forming a wave called a tidal bore. The record for the longest standing surf run here is 7.6 miles / 12.2 km which was made in 2006.

THE BIBLE SAYS . . .

'Where the word of a king is, there is power.' (Ecclesiastes 8:4) [Most true of God, the King of kings!]

'The Lord caused the [Red] sea to go back by a strong east wind ..., and made the sea dry land.' (Exodus 14:21)

OCEAN CURRENTS

Finding efficient trading routes in the seas and oceans

How a broken leg and a Bible verse have made most of us richer

Matthew Maury was a sailor in the United States Navy before the Civil War. At age 33 he broke his leg in a stagecoach accident and could not sail—it was vital to be able-bodied. He was confined to 'desk duty', doing only office work. However, this event was to change the future of shipping. Matthew had been raised with a knowledge of the Bible and having read Psalm 8:8 about 'paths of the seas,' he believed that this was speaking about ocean currents, where water flows from one region to another. He therefore set about studying all of the US Navy logbooks which had been stored away, to identify where ships had made good progress, and developed a uniform way of recording it all on charts. What emerged was a pattern of 'paths' which captains could follow to save a lot of time (and money) and make the most of favourable currents and winds. On his initiative, a maritime conference was held in Brussels, Belgium in 1853, and the charts were considered so valuable that afterwards some countries who were former enemies agreed to work together, sharing weather information and adopting an international standard of weather reporting. Ever since, shipping has sought to follow these 'paths in the seas.'

Matthew Maury was nicknamed 'Pathfinder of the Seas' and is considered the father of modern oceanography (ocean science)

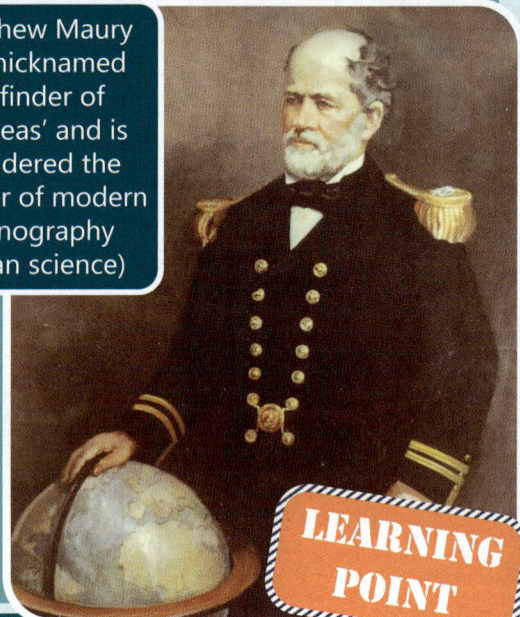

LEARNING POINT

What seemed like an unfortunate accident has benefitted the whole world; we are better off because Matthew Maury broke his leg. In the lives of Bible characters there were times of great difficulty, but the end result was one of great benefit for God's people; for example see Joseph (Genesis 50:20), Naomi (Ruth 4:14-17), Esther (Esther 10:3), and John (Revelation 1:9-11). Paul suffered all sorts of pain, but he was clear: God had used all of those trials to bring about much good. In particular, Jesus suffered more than we can imagine; but the benefit is Heaven for all who trust in Him.

THE BIBLE SAYS...
Paul wanted the early church to 'understand ... that the things which happened unto me have fallen out rather unto the furtherance [spreading] of the gospel.' (Philippians 1:12)

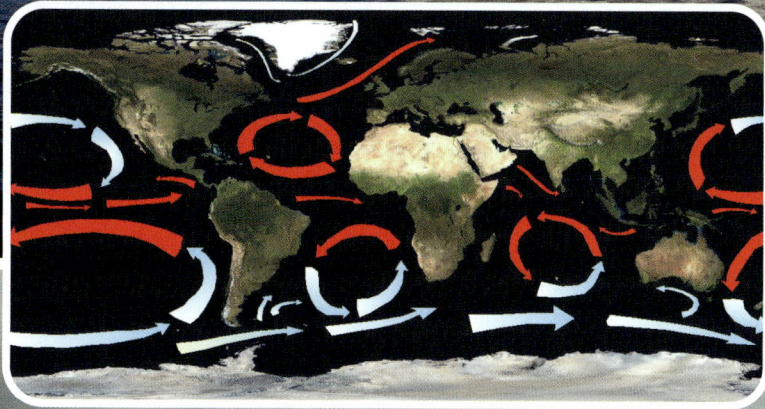

Whether a wind-powered sailing ship built for trade like this five-mast clipper (above), or a huge modern container ship powered by engines (below), shipping goes faster by following ocean currents (left). This saves time and money, which makes goods cheaper.

OIL AND GAS RIGS

Platforms to drill for energy under the sea bed

Cheap, abundant energy: a blessing or a curse?

Drilling for oil at sea started in earnest after World War 2, initially with rigs resting on the sea bed on long steel legs. As technology has improved, rigs have been set up in deeper water; it is now common to have rigs which float and are kept in position using computer-controlled thrusters. The *Perdido* is the deepest floating oil platform in the world at a water depth of 2450 meters (8040 feet). Oil and gas is either pumped ashore by pipeline or collected by a ship. It is a wonder of the modern age that petrol costs no more than premium bottled water (ignoring UK government fuel duty), despite the many processes for finding, extracting, refining, transporting and dispensing it.

Did you know that over the last 100 years, the risk of death due to climate-related disasters has dropped 98%? Why is this? It is because of cheap and reliable energy, which has made production of metal and concrete affordable, enabling more building work, helped also by cheap diesel to fuel construction vehicles. This has allowed construction of robust buildings strong enough to withstand floods, hurricane-force winds, and be earthquake-proof. Flood defences have also been built and crop-watering and drinking water treatment schemes defend against drought. Affordable energy heats homes to counter winter illness, and saves lives by powering hospitals. Cheap energy has also reduced the cost of food, so we have a super-abundance of it like never before.

80% of the world's energy comes from oil, gas and coal. Current governments are making fuel more scarce and expensive as they tackle what they say is a 'climate crisis' caused by Man burning too much carbon-rich fuel like oil and gas. However, these policies, without a switch to an alternative reliable fuel source (like nuclear?) will lead to more poverty and death, especially in the poorest countries, as they cannot match the prices which the US, UK and Europe can afford.

LEARNING POINT

At the time of writing, it seems that the opposition to using oil and gas is getting more intense. Protestors are full of enthusiasm and have a burning desire (zeal) to change the world for the better, as they see it, by averting a climate catastrophe. Arguably, the environment could be affected worse *without* oil and gas; it leads to people in poorer countries clearing and burning more rain forest and woodland, threatening more creatures with loss of their natural habitat, and so forth. And more people die when there is poverty. There is a zeal which can be misplaced, that is, it is not according to a proper knowledge of the truth (see

(above) Crew training on securing a well, Malaysia, 2016

(right) A Shell platform off the coast of Norway on a calm day

(below) A rig in for repair at Invergordon, near Inverness, Scotland, with truck for scale

Helicopter landing pad

Crane for loading to/from supply ships

Flare for burning off unwanted gas

Emergency escape pods

THE BIBLE SAYS ...
'Buy the truth, and sell it not; also wisdom, and instruction, and understanding.' (Proverbs 23:23)

'Give *me* an understanding heart ... that I may discern between good and bad.' (2 Kings 3:8-10)

Romans 10:2). How important it is not just to believe what we hear at school, work, or on the news, without looking at all sides of the argument. Something may seem right, but is it? (Proverbs 14:12, 16:25, 18:13, John 7:24). This principle is so important. Don't even believe everything you read in this book; check it for yourself (if you can get past internet censorship!). The Christians in Berea were praised by the Apostle Paul, because they were careful to check whether what the preacher said matched what was in the Old Testament scriptures. How important it is to discern the truth.

FISHING
Catching the 'fruit of the sea'

"What is your net worth?"

Fishing at sea has long been a way of coastal towns and villages feeding themselves and earning a good living. Fishermen have to be extremely resilient, able to withstand sea-sickness, hard physical work, strong smells, and the danger which comes from the unpredictable weather at sea. Commercial fishing vessels generally operate by dragging (trawling) one or more large weighted nets behind the boat, and then they are winched in to sort the catch. Modern vessels are fitted with sonar, which look down into the water to locate shoals of fish.

Fishermen have to cope with very poor weather—it isn't a job for the faint-hearted

Recent years have seen the use of 'factory ships.' These are big trawlers often 50-70m long with a crew of 35 or more, designed so that they can sort the catch, fillet it and freeze it for freshness and lowest cost. The largest factory ship is 144m long and its crew of 63 can catch and process 350-400 tonnes of fish a day, taking up to 7,000 tonnes of prepared frozen catch back to land.

LEARNING POINT

You probably know that Jesus told Peter, Andrew, James and John, who were fishermen, to leave their nets and follow Him. He said that He would make them 'fishers of men.' He meant by this that they would preach the Gospel (like throwing a net into the sea), and then some people would be 'caught', that is, they hear and keep going to church, as though they were drawn in a net. Jesus told many parables— earthly stories with a heavenly meaning. One of these is recorded for us in Matthew 13:47-50 and is about sea fishing. He said that the 'kingdom of heaven' is like a large net, which when dragged back to the shore, had all kinds of sea creatures and other stuff in it. The fishermen then sorted through the catch, putting the good into pots, and throwing away the bad. What did He mean by this? Jesus was saying that, at the end of the world, not everyone who goes to church or has been baptized will go to Heaven. How solemn! Only those who truly love Jesus; it is our *heart* that matters! (1 John 3)

THE BIBLE SAYS ...
Jesus said, 'No man can come to me, except the Father ... draw him.' (John 6:44)
Read Matthew 7:21-23

(right) Dutch trawler *LO 13 Stormvogel* showing the way it deploys a net on each side

(bottom left) A fisherman sorts the catch on trawler *African Queen*

Factory trawler *Akamalik* fishes for shrimp far from shore in the deep water of the North Atlantic

DID YOU KNOW?

Being a deep sea fisherman is the UK's most dangerous peacetime job; it is over 100 times more deadly than an average job

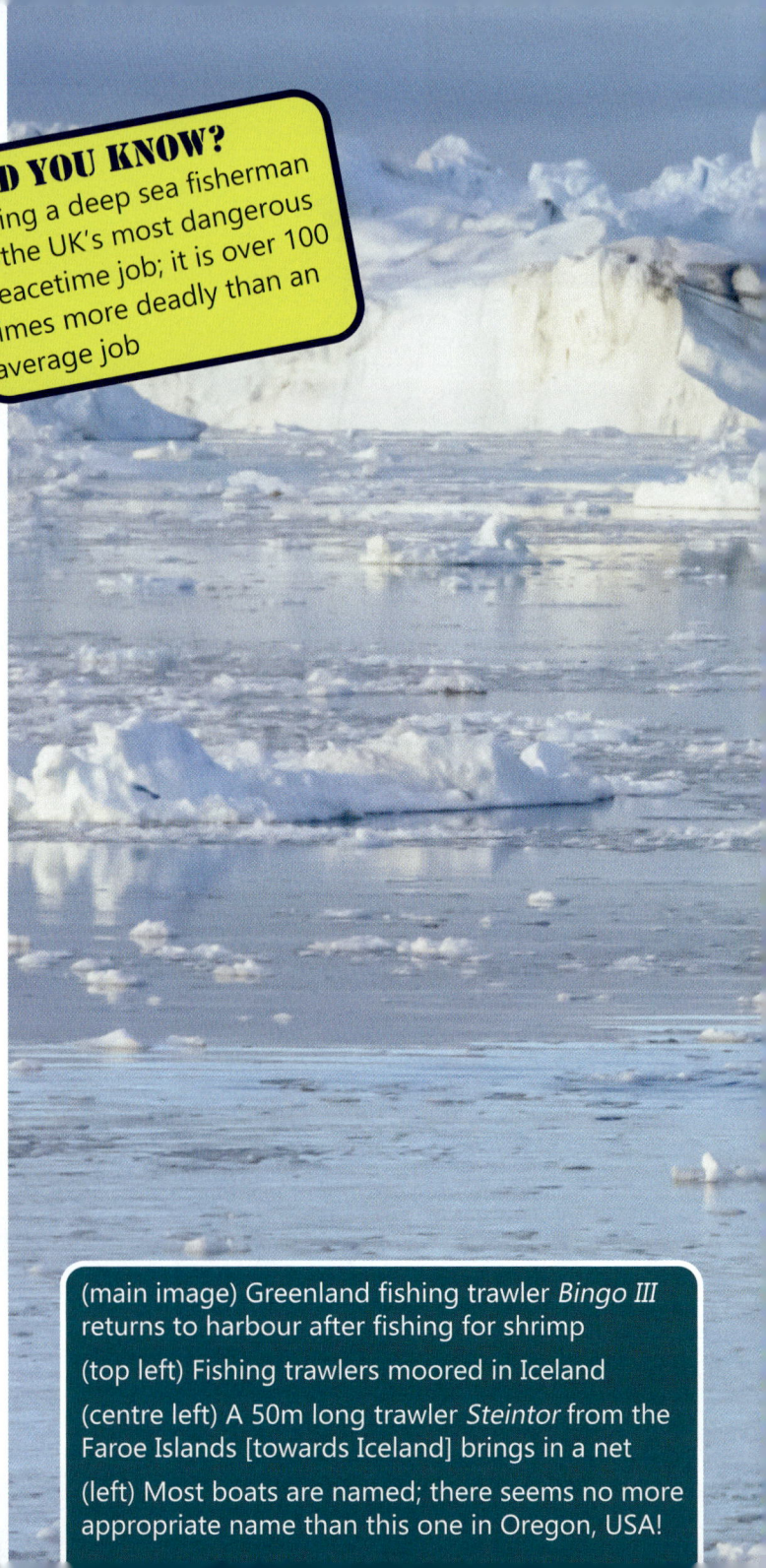

(main image) Greenland fishing trawler *Bingo III* returns to harbour after fishing for shrimp

(top left) Fishing trawlers moored in Iceland

(centre left) A 50m long trawler *Steintor* from the Faroe Islands [towards Iceland] brings in a net

(left) Most boats are named; there seems no more appropriate name than this one in Oregon, USA!

SCUBA DIVING
Self-Contained Underwater Breathing Apparatus

(right) The Red Sea is a popular place for scuba diving due to the warm, clear sea and abundant marine life

(below) Practicing emergency procedures in the safety of a swimming pool

Under the sea is where I like to be

Under the waves there is a whole world which we cannot see from above the surface. The oceans teem with wonderful sea creatures, and there are shipwrecks and coral reefs to explore. For centuries, diving was impractical for most, requiring holding your breath for a long time, until the invention of reliable diving bells in the early 1800s. Any system which relied on a tube feeding air to the diver from the surface was restrictive. All that changed between the mid-1800s and 1943 when equipment was gradually developed for divers, culminating in the introduction of the first modern 'SCUBA' gear developed by Jacques Cousteau and Émile Gagnan, known as the Aqua-Lung. Although this has been improved over time, modern scuba kit still comprises compressed air in a cylinder, fed into a mouthpiece or face mask. Divers are weighted down to stop them floating, and they wear flippers on their feet.

DID YOU KNOW?
Scuba diving is not to be confused with snorkelling, which uses a breathing tube only, not an air tank

Swimming with a dolphin

LEARNING POINT

Pearls are smooth, round, and shiny, and found within some shellfish. In Bible times these had to be obtained by 'free diving', that is, without use of any breathing kit as it hadn't been invented. The finest pearls are rare and, because of the need to dive, were hard to obtain in days gone by, and so have been (and still are) highly valued.

Jesus talked about a pearl of great price. What can this be, but Jesus Himself? The Bible says that He is 'altogether lovely' (Song of Solomon 5:16) and His words are better than gold and silver (Psalm 119:72). Are you or I like Moses, who was prepared to give up all the wealth around him, so he could be with God and His people? (Hebrews 11:26)

THE BIBLE SAYS...
'The kingdom of heaven is like a merchant seeking beautiful pearls, who, when he had found one pearl of great price, went and sold all that he had and bought it.' (Matthew 13:45-46)

SHARKS
Fearsome fish

A reconstruction of a jaw from a giant extinct shark named megalodon, in Kentucky, USA

In the jaws of death?

Sharks are incredible creatures. Pages of this book could be filled with the wonders of their design. Here are just a few of the things which make them miracles of Creation:

BODY TEMPERATURE HIGHER THAN THE SEA
Unlike most fish having only white muscle, Great Whites have red muscle in their core which produces heat, and a system of blood vessels like an industrial heat exchanger.

SLIPPERY SKIN (DERMAL DENTICLES)
Sharks have an outer skeleton of fibres which spiral around their body, to which their swimming muscles attach. It reduces turbulence, saving energy when swimming.

ABILITY TO CONTINUOUSLY REPLACE THEIR TEETH
Some sharks have several rows of teeth, which are continuously growing and moving forward to replace teeth worn or lost. Sharks can lose 30,000 teeth in their lifetime!

EXTREMELY SENSITIVE SMELL
Some can smell blood even if it is just one part per million (blood vs. seawater). They can detect the direction of a scent based on the timing of when it reaches each nostril.

THE BIBLE SAYS . . .
'The kings ... said to the ... rocks, Fall on us, and hide us ... from the wrath of the Lamb [Jesus].' (Revelation 6:15-16)

Jesus said, 'Fear not, little flock; for it is your Father's good pleasure to give you the kingdom.' (Luke 12:32)

A hammerhead shark

LEARNING POINT

Sharks have a reputation of being fearsome killers, and in a sense this is true. However, the actual danger that they pose to people is incredibly low, and we are at much more risk in everyday life, such as by crossing the road. As humans, we tend to fear the wrong things. What, or who, should we fear? See Luke 12:5-6 for the answer. There is a day coming when Almighty God will judge the living and the dead. The Bible says that even kings will want rocks to fall on them rather than face God. But there is hope. For any realising that they deserve God's wrath, there is forgiveness by trusting Jesus Christ. Christians truly have nothing to fear—not even death.

(main image) A great white shark attacking a fish lure off the coast of South Africa, 2016

(bottom x2) Diving in shark cages for protection, to get up close to great white sharks, off Guadalupe Island, in the Pacific Ocean off Mexico, 2014

DID YOU KNOW?
At 40 ft. / 12 metres long, (the length of a bus), whale sharks are the largest fish in the world

DID YOU KNOW?
In the USA, vending machines and cows each kill more people a year than do sharks

DEEP SEA CREATURES

Marine life thriving in the dark depths

DID YOU KNOW?
If Mt. Everest was put into the Marianas Trench (Mark 11:23!), it would still be 2km / 1.3 miles under water

The weird and the wonderful

Even today, 95% of the deep ocean has never been explored. Apart from the middle of an active volcano, it must be the harshest environment on Earth—freezing cold and pitch black, with a crushing pressure in the deepest parts 1,000 times greater than at the surface.

Can anything survive here? Incredibly the answer is, "Yes!" Even in the Marianas Trench, the deepest part of the ocean, researchers have found creatures including the snailfish. These animals have specially designed or adapted bodies which can cope with the pressure and cold. It is also common for creatures to grow to huge proportions, such as the colossal squid, the largest invertebrate in the world (i.e. without a backbone) which can weigh 500kg / 1,100 lb and be 10 metres / 33 ft. long. Being huge is actually an advantage at depths where food is scarce, as large animals have slower metabolism; that is, their bodies do not need as much food. It is estimated that a colossal squid could survive eating just one small fish a day (30g / 1.1oz.).

Below about 1,000 metres / 3,300 ft., the ocean is completely dark because sunlight doesn't reach that far down. In the eastern Pacific Ocean depths, three-quarters of marine creatures make their own light, sometimes to lure in other creatures for their next meal, or to confuse predators. They do this by making and mixing chemicals and enzymes. The dominant colours are blue and green, but some can produce red or yellow.

LEARNING POINT

Jonah thought that by running away from Israel to Tarshish, he could escape God. You know the rest of the story—he couldn't! Can we escape from God even in the darkest depths of the sea? No, He is there too (Psalm 139:7-10). This is good news for those who trust Jesus, because there is nowhere on Earth, in life or death, where God cannot reach and help His people.

A colossal squid washed up on a beach in Mexico, 2006

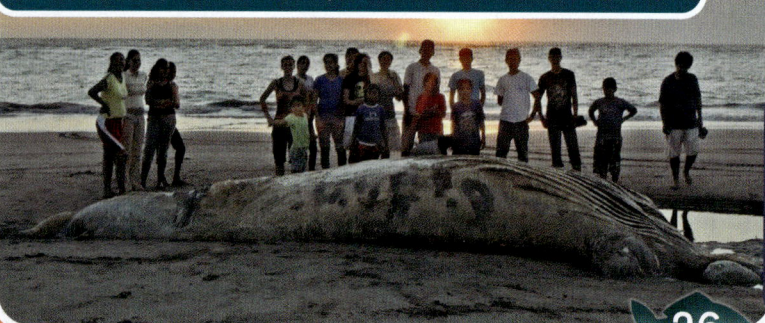

THE BIBLE SAYS . . .
'Neither death, nor life, nor height, nor depth, … shall be able to separate us from the love of God, which is in Christ Jesus our Lord.' (Romans 8:39)

In Micah 7:19, what does God say he will do with the sin of His people?

(right) A hydromedusa jellyfish, at a depth of 3,900m off the coast of Puerto Rico, central America

(inset) An octopus attaches to a deep sea submersible robot arm

(bottom) A ctenophore with tentacles extended to catch prey, at a depth of 1,460m / 4,800 ft. in the Gulf of Mexico

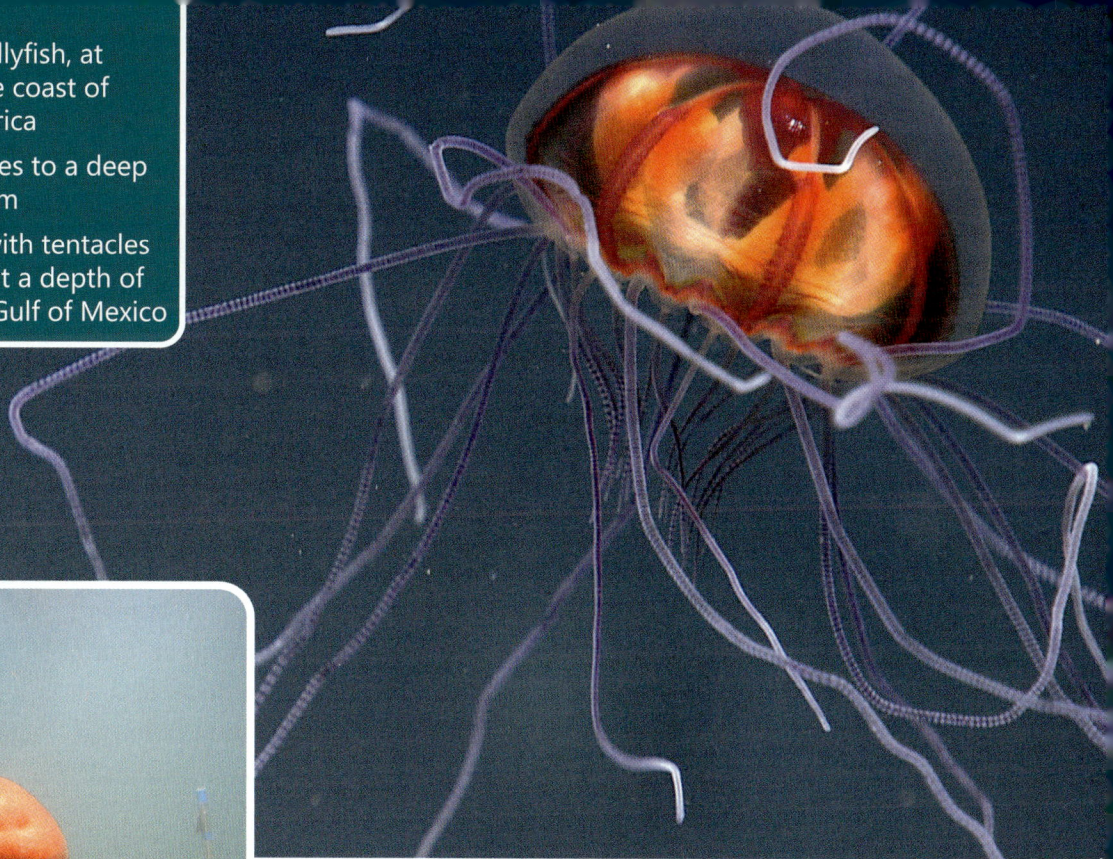

DID YOU KNOW?
The deepwater Greenland shark may live up to 500 years

SEA MONSTERS

Terrible sea creatures

Size comparison: The world's biggest great white shark, kronosaurus and a diver

The stuff of legends

For thousands of years, sailors have recounted stories of huge, and sometimes vicious, sea monsters. Almost everyone knows about the Loch Ness monster. These stories have been passed down to us as legends, and even reported in newspapers (see the 1848 London News article bottom right). In World War 1, a German submarine sunk a boat and when it sank there was an explosion, and the captain reported seeing a huge sea creature blown up into the air:

"The animal was about 20 metres [65 ft.] long and crocodile-like in shape, with pairs of strong front & hind legs adapted for swimming, and a long head that tapered towards the nose." According to the captain, the creature was visible for about "10 to 15 seconds at a distance of about 150-100 metres (500–300 ft.) in bright sunshine."

THE BIBLE SAYS . . .
God said about Leviathan, 'None is so fierce that [they would] dare stir him up: who then is able to stand before me?' (Job 41:10)

The people who argue most strongly against these stories are evolutionists. They agree that there have been massive sea creatures like kronosaurus (above)—we have fossil remains of their skeletons in museums—but they say they died out millions of years ago, so the stories cannot be true. Over the last 150 years, efforts to keep sea monster stories alive have been suppressed, as is recognised on the board shown to the right in a museum in Iceland.

LEARNING POINT

Can the Bible help us figure out fact from fiction? Yes! Did you know that in Job chapter 41, God gives a very detailed description of a fire-breathing sea monster which must have been commonly known at the time, presumably because of stories told by sailors. This beast, which God calls Leviathan, was the most fearless of all His Creation, and it was so vigorous that it made the ocean to froth like boiling water. It was such a terrifying sight, that brave mariners would wet themselves, and worse (Job 41:25 KJV).

Where are sea monsters now? Before the worldwide Flood of Noah's day, the Earth's environment was warmer and reptiles and dinosaurs found it easier to live. After the Flood, the climate cooled, and sea monsters just probably started dying out, and sightings would have started reducing as there were fewer of them. So, who knows? Maybe the falling waters after Noah's Flood left some sea monsters trapped in lakes, giving rise to legends like the Loch Ness monster.

A plesiosaur at the Houston Museum of Natural Science, USA. Plesiosaurs could be nearly 12m / 40 ft long.

An artist's impression: augustasaurus

Icelandic monsters

ders hav
althou
videnc
n as n
t eve
scripti
ng els
d as s
o stor

categorie
sh the
ng prog

d evalu
cument
ers bel
t comm
in lak

Almost every family in Iceland can relate unwritten ghost stories or descriptions of elves and hidden people, but monsters are something else. Anyone who says they have seen a monster is regarded as strange. This has led to monster tales being treated as taboo stories, and people no longer relate their experiences unless particularly asked to do so.

Monsters were treated as part of natural science until 1860. Jón Bjarnason from Þorormstunga wrote many natural science papers

Some of the many old illustrations of sea monsters before the 20th Century

THE ILLUSTRATED LONDON NEWS.

The great Sea-Serpent, according to different Descriptions

THE GREAT SEA-SERPENT.

An artist's impression of a plesiosaur (left) and a kronosaurus (lower right)

A reconstruction of a mosasaur skeleton at Cleveland Museum of Natural History, USA

An illustration of a mosasaur swimming in shallow water

"But surely this story cannot be true?"

There are many people including well-educated scientists who scoff at the idea that the worldwide flood recorded by Moses in Genesis 6-8 was a real event, despite the fact that the whole face of the Earth is covered in rock layers laid down by water, which are full of billions of dead things. The objections to the story of the ark are many. There is an amazing technical book called 'Noah's Ark: A Feasibility Study" by John Woodmorappe, which demonstrates how every aspect of the ark account is possible. One of the most remarkable things about the ark is that a 1993 study by marine scientists showed that the overall proportions of the ark were ideal, as it would have been strong, seaworthy in rough storms, and it was good for reducing sea-sickness. The ark is 6 times as long as it is wide, which is similar to modern tanker ships. Its design was so good, that the study estimated it could cope with waves 30 metres/100 ft. high! So if Moses made up Genesis out of his imagination, was it really just a coincidence that he got this vital detail right? I think not.

LEARNING POINT

Noah was given a design for building the ark, because God knew exactly how big it needed to be to accommodate all the animals and their food, and because He knew which wood and proportions would do the job best; He is all-wise. Noah carefully followed God's instructions (Genesis 6:22, 7:5)—not only did his life depend on it, but the lives of his family, and the future of mankind and the animal kingdom. Even more significant than that, mankind had to survive because the promised Saviour would one day be born of a woman.

The ark is often considered to be a picture of what God would do in saving sinners by His Son Jesus Christ. The ark was the only way to be saved from the Flood; and being found 'in' Jesus is the only way to escape God's wrath. The majority of people would not listen to Noah's warnings, in the same way that the majority today do not listen to the Gospel. The ark had just one door; likewise, the only way of salvation is in one way, through Jesus (John 10:9).

DID YOU KNOW?

The ancient Greeks made huge wooden ships (using Noah's know-how?) which were not surpassed in size until the iron-hulled *SS Great Eastern* in 1858

THE BIBLE SAYS . . .

Jesus said, 'I am the door: by me if any man enter in, he shall be saved.' (John 10:9)

Read 2 Peter 3:3-9 (Flood in v.6)

SHIP DESIGN
Making ships and boats safe and useful

All ship-shape

Ship building requires designers to take account of a large number of factors to build a ship that will be both safe and effective. Here are some of the main ones.

BUOYANCY
A hull shape which resists capsizing (see diagram opposite) and balances stability (wider hull) with speed (narrow hull)

CONTROL
A rudder (or 2) to steer the ship, and engines / thrusters which can be used to slow and manoeuvre the ship for docking

SAFETY
Good visibility from the bridge; navigation lights (avoid collisions); lifeboats; watertight compartments to resist flooding

COMFORT
Engines and propellors cause vibration if incorrectly designed; the ship design should seek to reduce seasickness

STRENGTH
Large waves can stress a ship by leaving some of it hanging in mid-air, so it could break in half unless built strongly

DURABILITY
Seawater will corrode metal and marine life can rot timber; use special paints, treatments or electrical protection

Bow (the ship's 'nose') *Fore* means towards the bow

Anchor

Bulbous bow to reduce drag

The *SCOT Augsburg*, on the New Waterway, Netherlands

Forward mast with navigation lights

Winch

Starboard (right hand side of ship)

Midships (the middle of a ship)

Forecastle (raised front deck) to deflect waves

Deck

Port (left hand side of ship)

Hull (the ship body providing the buoyancy)

Draught (depth of hull below water when laden)

Hold (the main cargo storage space in the hull)

Keel [not shown] (the backbone of the ship, the lowest structural beam running front to back)

SCOT-8000 CLASS
Safety Chemical and Oil Tanker
Length: 110m   Beam (width): 18m
Height: 9.4m   Draught: 7.4m
Load capacity (DWT): 8,000 tonnes
Speed: 16 knots / 30 kph
No. built: 12, Romania, 2002-2008

A cross-section through a ship. When it rolls to the right, the centre of buoyancy 'B' (the water pushing up against the ship) moves to the right. If the centre of gravity 'G' is to the left of 'B', it rights itself.

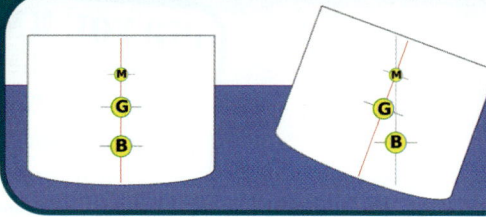

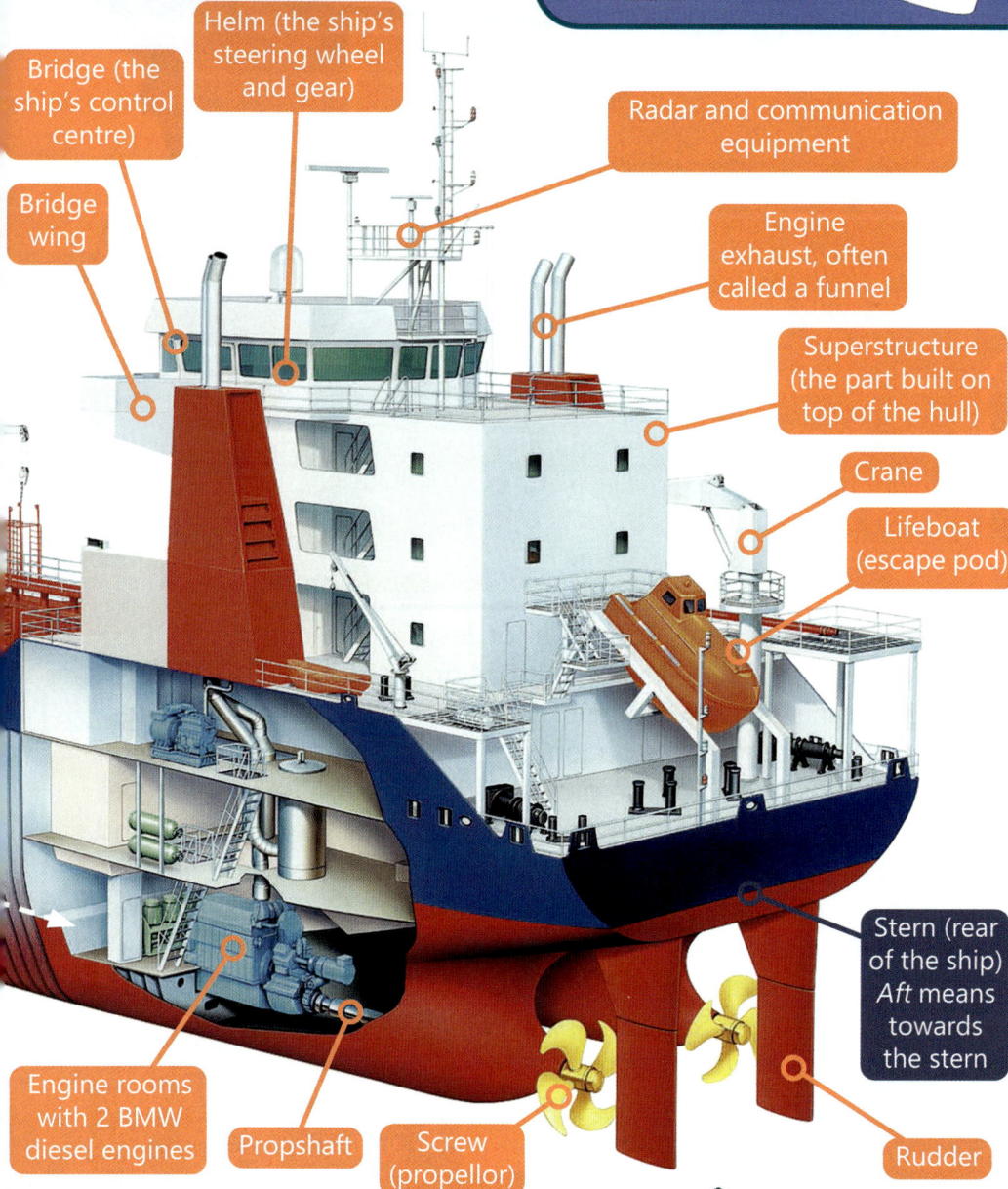

A ship's rudder is small compared with the size of the hull, but it can turn the ship around if the helmsman wishes. The Apostle James likens our *tongue* to a ship's rudder; our words can have a much bigger effect than we think! (Proverbs 18:21). What we say can hurt others and even ruin lives. Our words flow from what is in our heart which is corrupt by nature, so we often say wrong things (Matthew 15:11). But there is One whose words were **always** full of grace, because His heart was, and is, perfect. 'Never man spake like this man' (John 7:46). Jesus's words have changed the course of people's lives the world over. Have His words changed yours?

THE BIBLE SAYS...
The ships, which though they be so great ... yet are they turned about with a very small helm [rudder] ... so is the tongue among our members [body parts].' (James 3:4,6)

Bridge (the ship's control centre)

Helm (the ship's steering wheel and gear)

Bridge wing

Radar and communication equipment

Engine exhaust, often called a funnel

Superstructure (the part built on top of the hull)

Crane

Lifeboat (escape pod)

Stern (rear of the ship) *Aft* means towards the stern

Engine rooms with 2 BMW diesel engines

Propshaft

Screw (propellor)

Rudder

⚓ ANCHORS
Devices to stop a ship drifting off

Anchor chain

Heavy metal . . . very heavy!

After a means of steering and propulsion (power), arguably the next most important thing on a boat or ship is an anchor. It is so important that ships are normally fitted with two, in case one doesn't work. It is connected to a chain and dropped from a ship to stop it drifting off when it is moored. Usually this is close to a port when it is waiting to enter. It is shaped so that it digs into the seabed if it is dragged along. It is normal to let out a length of chain 7 times as deep as the water, so that when the boat moves about in the water, the heavy chain can absorb energy, stopping the anchor moving.

A traditional fluked anchor (flukes are the pointed 'teeth'

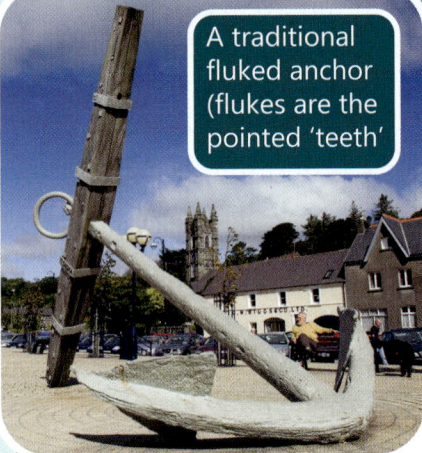

Anchors have traditionally been made of wood with metal (such as lead and iron) since at least the time of Christ, but modern anchors are made entirely of steel. There are many different designs, but they all have the same purpose.

LEARNING POINT

Christians can find it hard to live for Jesus in the world, because Satan stirs up a lot of opposition, like a rough sea tossing a ship. Fallen human nature also makes believers 'drift off' and stop looking to Jesus for all needed help. What guards against these problems? It is a sure **hope**—a belief that what God has said is true, and therefore all His promises about the forgiveness of sin, and the glory that awaits believers in Heaven, will most definitely come true (Psalm 85:2, Luke 23:43, John 14:2). The Apostle Paul says that this hope is like an anchor which is *firmly fixed*. It ties Christians to Jesus their Saviour. *This* is an anchor which prevents drifting off, no matter the situation!

Will your anchor hold in the storms of life,
when the clouds unfold their wings of strife?
When the strong tides lift, and the cables strain,
will your anchor drift, or firm remain?

We have an anchor that keeps the soul steadfast and sure while the billows roll;
fastened to the Rock which cannot move,
grounded firm and deep in the Saviour's love!

Priscilla Owens 1829-1907

THE BIBLE SAYS . . .
'Lay hold upon the hope set before us: which hope we have as an anchor of the soul, both sure and stedfast.' (Hebrews 6:18-19)

The port anchor is dropped on the *USS Ronald Reagan*, a nuclear-powered Nimitz class aircraft carrier, 2005

(below) The *USS Ronald Reagan* drops her 27-tonne starboard anchor in Japan, 2008

(below left) Painting the anchor on the *USS Dwight D. Eisenhower* in Virginia, USA, 2017

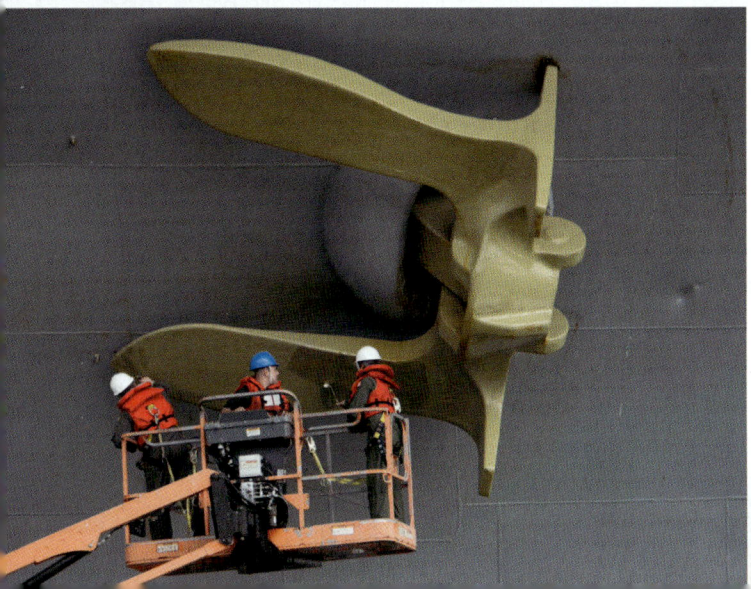

STORMS AT SEA

Howling winds, driving rain, and waves like cliffs

Wanted: Nerves of steel, good seamanship and humility

All seafarers must get used to riding out storms at sea. On the open ocean, there are no hills or trees to slow the wind, so its energy goes into the sea by whipping up waves (Psalm 107:25). If the wind blows strongly for long enough and far enough (a long "fetch"), waves can grow to 12 metres high (40 ft.) or more in places like the west coast of Ireland. That is the height of a 4 storey building! Efforts are made to angle ships relative to the waves to avoid capsizing.

For centuries, sailors have told stories of huge, towering waves, far bigger than the 12 metre waves often encountered at sea. However, these accounts of enormous 'rogue waves' were dismissed as just exaggerated tales for many years. More recently though, evidence has amassed about these waves, including damage to major ocean-going liners such as the *QE2*:

> **"The rogue wave was sighted right ahead, looming out of the darkness from 220°, it looked as though the ship was heading straight for the white cliffs of Dover. The wave seemed to take ages to arrive ... before it broke with tremendous force over the bow. An incredible shudder went through the ship ... The second wave of 28-29 m (period 13 seconds), whilst breaking, crashed over the foredeck, carrying away the forward whistle mast."** *11 September 1995*

LEARNING POINT

Here we see the power of God and the weakness of Man. Mariners have long feared the tempestuous sea and called on the LORD to spare them from a watery grave—read Psalm 107:23-31 and Jonah 1. Even with all his technology and skilful seamanship, Man cannot guarantee safety at sea, let alone end a storm. But there is One who is mightier than a tempest—the Lord Jesus Christ. He stopped the raging Sea of Galilee with the words, 'Peace, be still', and then the Bible says, 'the wind ceased, and there was a great calm.' We know this was a miracle because when the wind dies, there is still energy in the water causing waves (called "swell"). It is a blessing if, when we read this account, we can join with the disciples and say, "What manner of man is this, that even the wind and the sea obey him?"

Be still, my soul; the waves and winds still know
His voice who ruled them while He dwelt below
Kathrina von Schlegel 1697-1797

A large wave towering astern the US research ship *Delaware II* in the Atlantic Ocean, 2005

(below) In 1943 the *RMS Queen Mary*, one of the biggest and fastest ocean liners, was carrying 11,300 US troops and crew when it was hit in the side by a 28m / 92 ft. wave. She rolled over 52 degrees, nearly capsizing. It could have been the worst maritime disaster in history.

(right) A small ship totters on a huge wave in the Bering Sea, Alaska

Eternal Father, strong to save,
Whose arm hath bound the restless wave,
Who biddest the mighty ocean deep
Its own appointed limits keep;
    Oh, hear us when we cry to Thee,
    For those in peril on the sea!

O Christ, whose voice the waters heard
And hushed their raging at Thy Word,
Who walked on the foaming deep,
And calm amidst its rage didst sleep;
    Oh, hear us when we cry to Thee,
    For those in peril on the sea!

Most Holy Spirit, who didst brood
Upon the chaos dark and rude,
And bid its angry tumult cease,
And give, for wild confusion, peace;
    Oh, hear us when we cry to Thee,
    For those in peril on the sea!

O Trinity of love and power,
Our family shield in danger's hour;
From rock and tempest, fire and foe,
Protect us wheresoever we go;
    Thus evermore shall rise to Thee
    Glad hymns of praise from land and sea.

This hymn by William Whiting, first published in
1861, was inspired by Psalm 108 and references
God the Father's promise not to flood the Earth
again (Genesis 9:11, Psalm 104:9), Jesus's power
in stilling the storm on the Sea of Galilee and
walking on its water (Matthew 8:23-27, 14:22-33),
and the Spirit's part in the original creation of the
world (Genesis 1:2). It has been varied many times
and adopted by the Royal Navy and US Navy.

Karsten's ship, the 160m long tanker M/T Stolt Surf

A dramatic series of photographs by Danish marine engineer Karsten Petersen taken during a hurricane in the Pacific Ocean, October 1977. He recounts the storm:

"We experienced to our astonishment, that when the big waves came crashing towards us, we had to look UP in order to see the top of the waves! And that was from the bridge deck ... Several times we experienced huge waves coming crashing OVER the bridge,- more than 22 meters up -, and in some very, very long seconds we only saw sea water through the bridge windows, while tons of water ran off the bridge roof... In those terrible moments we did not know if the ship was below the water or still floating! But like a miracle the windows cleared again, - and "Stolt Surf" continued its brave battle against the waves.

"Of course the ship suffered quite a lot of damage that showed the incredible force of the water. Three of the solid tank hatches on deck were simply torn off, and so was the door to the pump room, in spite of the fact that such a door is made of steel... Straight pipelines on deck were now S-shaped, - and likewise the gangways, which was found as a mess of folded and twisted metal.

"Inside, all decks except the deck just below the bridge were filled with water through smashed windows and doors, and the crashing waves smashed furniture and wall paneling to pulp... The electricity supply to many parts of the accommodation was knocked out as well, so the cook had to prepare food for 35 men on a single portable cooking plate, but never had a meal tasted better on any ship!"

SHIPWRECKS
Sunken, grounded or beached vessels

USS Buchanan sinks after being used as target practice, near Hawaii, 2000

When ships are broken or damaged

From the earliest days of sailing, ships have been sunk, dashed against rocks, or grounded. Some causes of shipwreck are listed below. Sometimes ships are sunk on purpose; they make good artificial reefs for marine life.

COMMON CAUSES OF SHIPWRECK
Swamped with or capsized by waves
Loss of power or control, drifting onto rocks
Driven by fierce winds
Lack or loss of awareness of ship's position
Miscalculating sea depth vs. vessel 'draught'
Lack of knowledge of the coast and hazards
Reckless or careless behaviour by the crew
Collision with another vessel (or iceberg)
Poor design or badly loaded (unstable)
Fire; or intentional damage e.g. pirates, war

Historians are interested in shipwrecks because they reveal much about life in the past and may tell us how the ship sank. They may also be of interest to treasure hunters, as riches were plundered from the Americas at the time of the European empires and transported back by ship, some of which sank. They are also of general interest for divers.

Shipwrecks sometimes cause local environmental damage; the Exxon Valdez ran aground off Alaska in 1989 spilling 37,000 tonnes of oil into the sea.

LEARNING POINT

Most ships are built with this purpose—to get across the sea to a destination, **safely**. If a vessel becomes shipwrecked, it will not get there! It will be either stranded or sunk. Even today, it is only relatively rare that a ship is recovered <u>and</u> re-used; the cruise ship Costa Concordia (right) was salvaged but then scrapped as it was heavily damaged.

The Christian's life is often likened to a sea voyage. The destination harbour is Heaven itself. The stormy waves are the difficulties of life, and rocks are like temptations. There is danger, and if a Christian has to steer his or her own ship, the result will be shipwreck. But there is a skilful *pilot* to help. (A pilot is an expert ship captain who steers it through dangerous waters, and who has detailed local knowledge.) Of course, this pilot is Jesus Christ as He is revealed in the words of the Bible. If Christians do their own thing, and are not looking wholly to Jesus every day, they are said to be at risk of shipwreck. Thankfully, not to the complete loss of the vessel! Jesus is ready to save everyone in need who cries unto Him (Psalm 86:7).

THE BIBLE SAYS...
'Holding faith, and a good conscience; which some having put away concerning faith have made shipwreck.' (1 Timothy 1:19)

Shipwreck of *MV Alta*; which was adrift in the Atlantic Ocean for two years without a crew, until it ran aground off Ireland in 2020

(above) The semi-submerged *Costa Concordia* which sank in 2012, claiming 32 lives, with 4,300 saved

(below) The *Exxon Valdez* after it ran aground, Prince William Sound

(right) Diving to an unknown wreck

Paul and Luke

In the Acts of the Apostles, we find the story of how the Gospel was spread by the Apostles after Jesus went back up to Heaven. They travelled around preaching and setting up churches. Paul went on at least three missionary journeys around the Mediterranean Sea, requiring him to take shipping. On his final voyage to Rome, he was shipwrecked with his companion Luke, who recorded all the details (in Acts 27), giving us a first-hand account of what it was like.

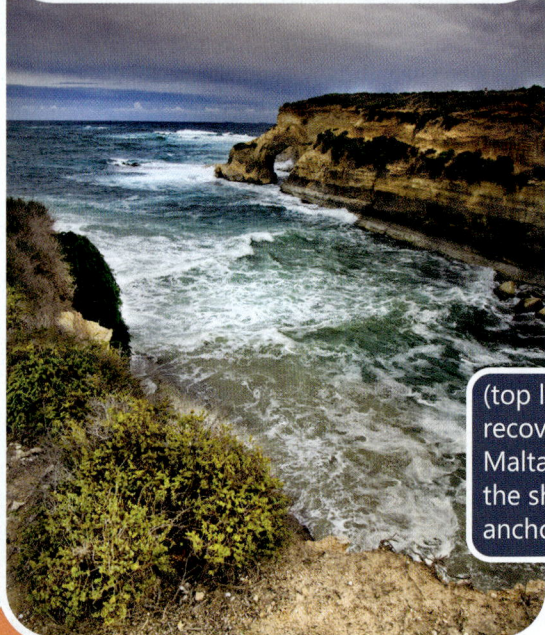

The ship was caught in a terrifying storm so fierce that they had to wrap ropes around the bottom of the ship to prevent it being torn apart, and as they could not hope to use the sails, they threw all of the equipment overboard with their cargo in a desperate bid to avoid sinking. Luke records that the weather was so bad that, after many days of being in this tempest, "All hope that we should be saved was taken away." However, an angel of God appeared to Paul in a dream with a message that Paul would certainly reach Rome, and everyone on board would survive this ordeal. So Paul relayed this to everyone on the ship, and they were filled with hope. The ship ran aground just off the coast of Malta, where it broke up and everyone had to swim to the shore or float there on boards amongst the stormy waves.

Paul records that he suffered shipwreck three times, and once he was floating in the 'deep' for about 24 hours before he was rescued (2 Corinthians 11:25). He knew the suffering of being shipwrecked. And yet he was determined to carry on travelling, preaching about Jesus Christ, no matter the risk!

(top left) An anchor from this time period is recovered, and (left) a part of St Thomas' Bay, Malta, in my opinion a good candidate for the shipwreck site. It is said that four Roman anchors were found here (see Acts 27:29,40).

Reflect on Paul's attitude in Acts 20:23-24

Horatio and Anna Spafford

Do you know the story of Job? He was a wealthy man who suddenly lost virtually everything (read Job 1:13-2:10). In the 1870s in America, there was a Christian, Horatio Spafford, who must have been able to sympathise with Job. Although a wealthy lawyer, he lost his fortune in a fire and then his young son died of illness. Not long after, in 1873, he planned a trip to Great Britain, but business delayed him so he sent his wife and four daughters on ahead on the *S.S. Ville du Havre*. On the journey, the ship collided with another, and sank in only 12 minutes, drowning all four of his daughters. His poor wife was rescued and, on reaching Wales, sent a short telegram message to her husband who had not heard about the tragedy. It read: **"Saved alone. Your wife."**

He was greatly moved by this sad loss of his four daughters, and wrote the well-known hymn, "It is well with my soul." It expresses something of the peace which Christians can have in terrible times of suffering and loss, because *eternal* life is much more precious than a relatively short life on the Earth.

Horatio and Anna Spafford, and their four young girls who drowned: Annie, Maggie, Bessie and Tanetta

Reflect on how Job and Eli reacted to trials; see Job 1:21, 1 Samuel 3:18

The Steam Ship (S.S.) *Ville du Havre*

When peace, like a river, attendeth my way,
When sorrows like sea billows* roll;
Whatever my lot, Thou has taught me to say,
It is well, it is well, with my soul.
> It is well, with my soul,
> It is well, it is well, with my soul.

Though Satan should buffet, though trials
  should come,
Let this blest assurance control,
That Christ has regarded my helpless estate,
And hath shed His own blood for my soul.

My sin, oh, the bliss of this glorious thought!
My sin, not in part but the whole,
It was nailed to his cross, and I bear it no more,
Bless the Lord, bless the Lord, O my soul!

2 Kings 4:26; Psalm 146:1   * large waves

THE TITANIC
The most infamous maritime disaster in history

Pride goes before destruction . . .

Sailing across the North Atlantic in wooden sailing ships was dangerous, given the frequent violent storms, huge waves and icebergs. When metal ships were introduced with powerful steam engines, it seemed as though Man was at last getting the mastery of the sea which had claimed so many lives. By 1910, confidence in ship design was at an all-time high. The White Star Line ordered three huge new ships, intended to be the most luxurious in the world. One of these was *Titanic*, the world's largest ship at that time; with 10 deck levels and 3 steam engines weighing 700 tonnes each. These engines were supplied with steam from 29 boilers, heated by 159 furnaces, using 600 tonnes of coal a day, shovelled in by 176 men. She was fitted with water-tight compartments in the hull, so a hole would not cause water to swamp the lower decks and sink it. The ship owners were confident that this huge ship was more than a match for the sea:

"There is no danger that *Titanic* will sink," boasted Philip Franklin, White Star Line vice president. "The boat is unsinkable and nothing but inconvenience will be suffered by the passengers."

You probably know the story; on its maiden voyage, it glanced an iceberg in the dark moonless night, gashing the hull in several places. The ship hadn't been designed to survive so many of the watertight compartments being flooded. It filled with water, and after 2 hours 40 minutes it sank with the loss of 1,500 lives. It is still the deadliest peacetime sinking of a liner or cruise ship.

LEARNING POINT

Nature's power is often seen at sea. How foolish for men to think that they can overcome nature, and downplay its awesome force! Is our confidence in scientists, engineers, the military and politicians? Or is it in the God who made everything, and holds all nature in His hands (Job 38:4-11, Psalm 65:7 and 89:9)? Nowadays we hear much about 'pride'. We may be told to be proud of our achievements, and even be encouraged to feel pride for things that are shameful. Solomon said that pride leads to destruction (Proverbs 16:18-19). It is far better to be humble, but how much do we hear about that? What an example was the Lord Jesus on the Earth. If anyone had a right to be proud, it was Him! But no. What does Jesus say of Himself in Matthew 11:29?

THE BIBLE SAYS . . .

'A man's pride shall bring him low: but honour shall uphold the humble in spirit.' (Proverbs 29:23)

'The pride of life, is not of the Father, but is of the world.' (1 John 2:16)

(top left, top right) The size of Titanic and her sister ships is clearly seen out of water; note the man circled yellow

(bottom right) The bow of the Titanic 3,700m / 2.3 miles below the waves

WHITE STAR LINE

DID YOU KNOW?
The Titanic's rudder weighed over 100 tonnes

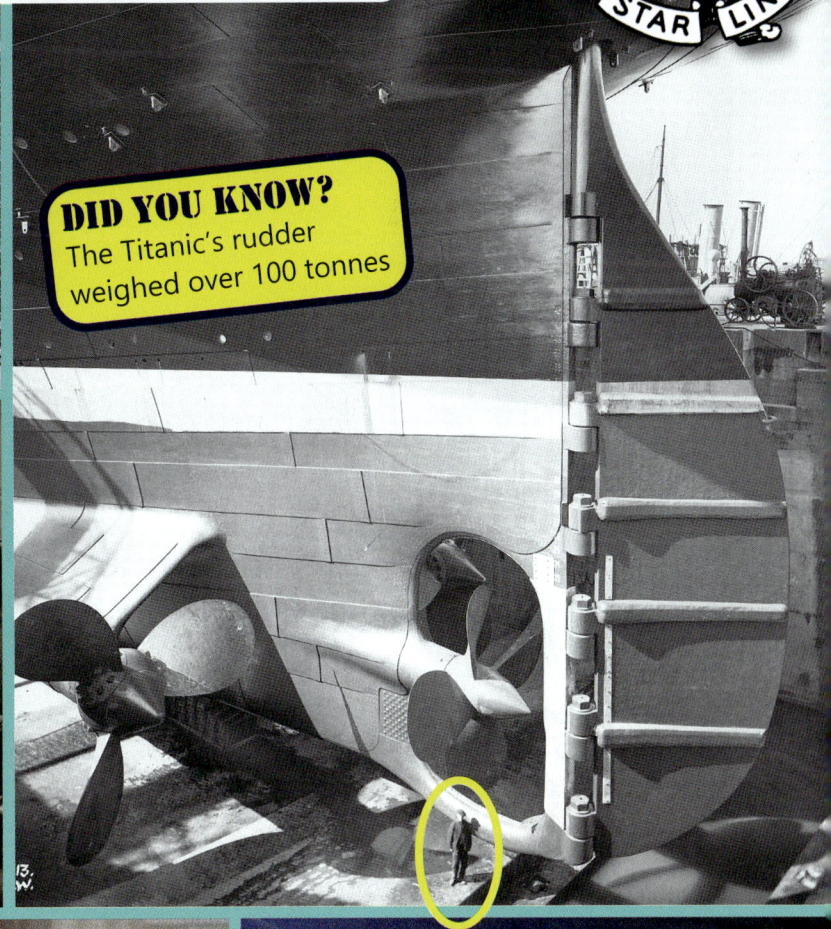

Departing Southampton on her first and final voyage towards New York, USA

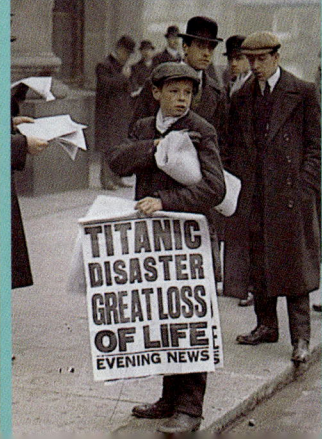

TITANIC DISASTER GREAT LOSS OF LIFE
EVENING NEWS

LIFE PRESERVERS

Rings, vests, rafts and boats to help you stay alive in the sea

What no-one wants to hear: "Abandon ship!"

Historically sailing ships carried small boats to allow their crew to get ashore when there was no dock available. These doubled as lifeboats if the ship was in danger (see Acts 27:30-32). By the time of the Titanic, lifeboats had to be carried on large ships by law. Early lifeboats were just wooden rowing boats, and they easily overturned in rough seas, or were accidentally dropped when lowered, which was deadly. With a bad reputation, fear led to some of *Titanic's* lifeboats being launched half-empty as people preferred to wait for rescue on board the 'unsinkable' ship. Ironically there have also been deaths *due* to lifeboats, such as the *Eastland* disaster near Chicago in 1915; after the *Titanic* sank, a new law required <u>more</u> lifeboats to be carried. The *Eastland's* owners hadn't considered the extra weight, and the ship capsized as it was top-heavy, killing 844 people.

It wasn't until 1943 that enclosed self-righting lifeboats were invented, forming the pattern for modern ship-borne lifeboats. Ships now often carry an array of life saving equipment such as rings, lifevests and inflatable rafts, which you can spot on the deck, under seating or fixed against railings or panels.

LEARNING POINT

Survival, or self-preservation, is a natural instinct (Ephesians 5:29). However, our natural instinct isn't always right. Look at what happened with the Titanic passengers who understandably wouldn't take to lifeboats when they had the opportunity. For some, this cost them their life. This may remind us of something which Jesus said, which may seem very strange—that those who try and save their life shall lose it, and those who lose their life shall keep it. What could this mean? Those who die to their old life, suffering hardship and shame because they follow Jesus and trust Him alone for salvation, have *eternal* life. Everyone who tries to save themselves, or live in ease, will not.

Opposite page:

(top left, inset) A cruise ship's lifeboats with room for 150 people each are tested monthly

(top right) Brave enough to get into this lifeboat? *USS Louisiana*, US Navy, c1920s

(centre left) Lifejackets

(centre right) Floats doubling as seating on the Mersey ferry

(bottom left) Training for inflatable life rafts, and (bottom right) a life raft in a canister

THE BIBLE SAYS . . .

'Whosoever shall seek to save his life shall lose it; and whosoever shall lose his life shall preserve it.' (Luke 17:33)

8 PERSONS

RESCUE AT SEA

Saving souls, whatever the weather

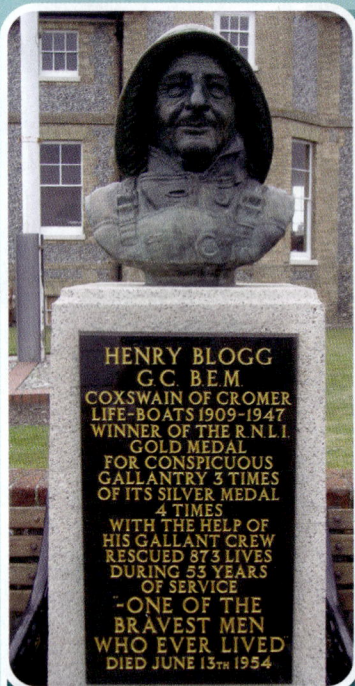

A memorial for Henry Blogg in Cromer, Norfolk

Only the brave

Did you know that around the shores of the UK and Ireland, there are over 250 lifeboat stations manned mostly by **volunteers**? That's right! Men and women who put their lives at risk to launch into rough seas and storms, if required, to rescue those in peril on the sea or around the coast. The first lifeboat organisation in the world, the Royal National Lifeboat Institution (RNLI), has saved over 140,000 people since 1824. Together with independent lifeboat organisations and the Royal Navy, Royal Air Force and HM Coastguard, rescue services are provided 24 hours a day, 365 days a year around the coast of Great Britian (and Ireland).

Arguably the most famous lifeboat rescue of all time was by 22 year old Grace Darling and her father, from the Longstone lighthouse on the Farne Islands in Northumberland in 1838. They rowed out to rescue stranded survivors after their ship broke up on the rocks in gale force winds. She became an overnight celebrity, although she was humble and didn't want the attention. It did much to raise awareness about the importance of lifeboats, and since then lifeboat services have spread around the world.

The RNLI sailor who has won the most medals for bravery is Henry Blogg (1876-1954). He served until he was 71 years old and, with his crew, saved 873 lives.

LEARNING POINT

How thankful we should be that there are volunteers who put their life on the line to save others. They don't do it for money, and often they are unknown to most, yet they still do it. Lifeboat volunteers may remind us of the voluntary choice of One who left the comfort of His dwelling place to enter the rough seas of life in a fallen world, to rescue those utterly unable to save themselves. He was so committed that He was prepared to suffer more than we can imagine, and was willing to die to accomplish the rescue. Yes, Jesus Christ the Son of God. He was successful (John19:30)—indeed, He could not fail!

THE BIBLE SAYS . . .
'The life I now live ... I live by the faith of the Son of God, who loved me, and gave himself for me.' (Galatians 2:20)

(above) Helicopters also play an important role; here a Royal Air Force Sea King moves in to winch an injured sailor off a fishing trawler in atrocious weather in the Irish Sea, 2013

(below) The crew of *RNLB Grace Darling* return into Seahouses harbour in their Mersey Class lifeboat after an exercise, 2009

(above) Henry Freeman was the only survivor after the Whitby lifeboat capsized in 1861, saved thanks to a cork lifejacket. He went on to serve as coxswain for 20 years, saving 300 lives.

(left) The 47-foot MLB (motor lifeboat) is the US Coastguard's main search-and-rescue vessel. It self-rights and can operate in winds up to 50 knots and waves of up to 30 feet / 9 metres high.

(right) A Tamar Class all-weather lifeboat splashes into the sea from its slipway at the Lizard, Cornwall, on an exercise, 2012

Robert is now an Archdeacon for the Church in Wales living in Criccieth, where he is part of the lifeboat crew, but he used to be the Vicar in Beaumaris, which is where this story starts...

A news report on one cold Monday evening in November 2019 about a missing person at sea led the concerned vicar to the RNLI lifeboat station to offer his prayers for the rescue.

While the crew were grateful for his prayerful support, they also needed more practical help and it took just a week to persuade Robert to join them as a member of the volunteer crew for their inshore lifeboat.

Today, as he has done for over 3 years, Robert keeps a life-jacket at hand as he combines his ministry with his RNLI role.

"Back on that cold November night, I didn't realise that the RNLI is always on the lookout for new volunteers, especially when they live and work so close to the lifeboat station," says Robert. "I was asked if I could come back to have a chat with the Lifeboat Operations Manager. He is a volunteer, as is everyone at the lifeboat station. Volunteers are all sorts of people, some who work on boats, others have limited experience of boats and the sea before they join.

"That Thursday chat ended up with me volunteering to become a member of the shore crew. I was given a pager [a device to receive messages] and started my training, all led by volunteers from the local lifeboat crew. Four months later, I had completed the shore-crew training and assessments, which included some new skills, like learning how to tie a number of knots!"

A lifeboat is launched from its trailer using a tractor, in Looe, Cornwall; this is something Robert has done for the Beaumaris lifeboat

"I've been part of the team on many shouts and nothing can prepare you for the sheer panic when a text message comes through for the first time!" says Robert. "You drop everything you're doing, respond to the message and proceed directly to the lifeboat station, not knowing what the shout is or how long you're going to be out for. Shouts can be boats breaking free of their moorings, breaking down, or something more serious,

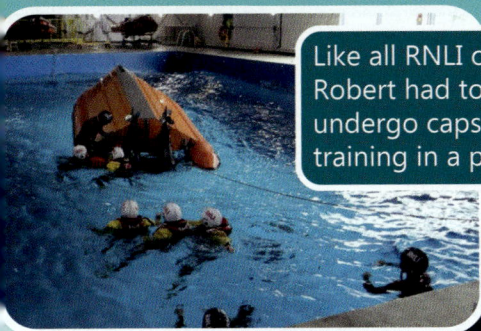

Like all RNLI crew, Robert had to undergo capsize training in a pool

A 'B Class' Atlantic lifeboat similar to the one on which Robert serves; these are some of the fastest lifeboats in service with the RNLI; they can do 35 knots / 65 kph

where lives can truly be in danger.

"I've also learnt to drive the tractor and trailer which launches and recovers the lifeboat. I've driven the tractor into the sea in the middle of a dark and windy night and been buffeted by the waves. The power of water is never to be underestimated.

"I've now also completed my training as a member of the crew on the lifeboat. I've learned about navigation at sea, radar and a host of other things, including going to the RNLI College in Poole to do sea safety and capsize training."

While driving launch tractors and jumping in lifeboats may seem a million miles away from leading worship, for Robert both are about his ministry as a Christian and service to others.

"As a Christian, sharing and showing Jesus' love is what motivates me, and if I then can help other people to see God at work, even better. For me, being a volunteer with the RNLI is about sharing and showing Jesus' love for others, by being one small cog in a community volunteer team which helps other people when they really need it. It also enables me to be involved in local community life.

"Jesus knew about boats, nets, fishing, wind and stormy seas, and as I learn more about the tides and waters around the Menai Straits, it opens up a whole new way of sensing God's presence through creation. If I can learn and realise more about God as I'm part of a team that helps and serves other people in a time of need, then volunteering with the RNLI is a really worthwhile thing to do."

From a 2020 Church in Wales article, updated with thanks to Robert Townsend

LIGHTHOUSES

Beacons which are the difference between life and death

Shining light into the darkness

While having an effective rescue service at sea is a wonderful provision, it is much better to avoid a shipwreck in the first place! Lighthouses are special structures designed to house a bright lamp in a very visible location, where there is danger of ships running aground in the dark on rocks or sandbanks.

Modern lighthouses are fully electric and the light from the bulbs is concentrated into narrow beams by a cleverly designed glass lens called a Fresnel lens, named after its inventor Frenchman Augustin-Jean Fresnel (1788–1827). This distinctive-looking lens is much lighter than a typical glass lens, allowing it to be rotated by a motor, giving rise to the flashes that you see when you look at a lighthouse. Each lighthouse has its own pattern of flashes so mariners can work out their location.

There are now more than 18,600 lighthouses world-wide and it has been said that a million ships have been saved from shipwreck.

The first ever lighthouse, built c 250 B.C., was at Alexandria in Egypt and was one of the Seven Wonders of the Ancient World; it stood 150m / 450 feet tall. It was destroyed by earthquake and invaders. The oldest one surviving is the Tower of Hercules in Spain, built c 20 A.D.

THE BIBLE SAYS...
'For God, who commanded the light to shine out of darkness, *has* shined in our hearts, to give the light of the knowledge of the glory of God in the face of Jesus Christ.' (2 Corinthians 4:6)

LEARNING POINT

If a preacher is faithful—that is, if he preaches the whole truth of the Bible as Jesus did, including the bits people don't like to hear—he will be like a lighthouse. A lighthouse sends a clear signal to warn of danger. There <u>is</u> danger; every man, woman and child has broken God's holy law, and there will be ruin unless they change direction.

To be saved, we need God's Word, centred in Christ the Saviour of sinners, to shine as a light into our dark hearts, and make Jesus precious to us (1 Peter 2:7). How can we see this Light (John 8:12) unless the Gospel is preached? (1 Corinthians 1:21). What a blessing to see the Light!

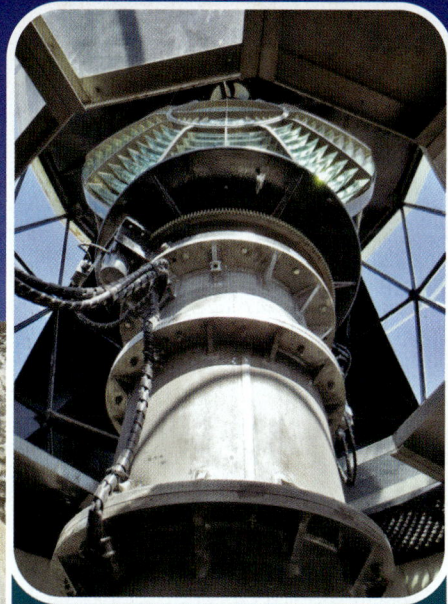

A Fresnel lens is seen here at the top of the photo, mounted on a turntable; the electric motor rotates it by driving the large toothed ring

Lighthouses are often tall, narrow, circular structures which are known for having long sets of spiral steps

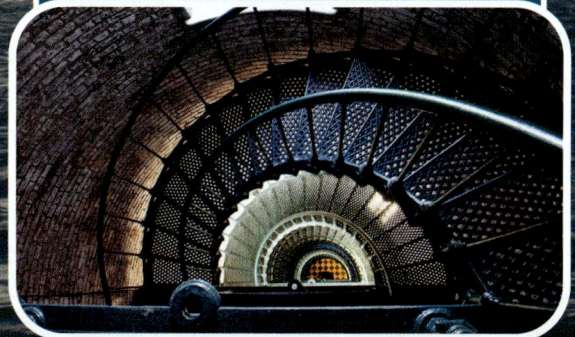

(main image) Beachy Head lighthouse, near Eastbourne, Sussex, UK; it was undergoing maintenance at the time—note the workman half way up

DID YOU KNOW?
'Daymarks' are the contrasting colours applied to help sailors identify lighthouses during the day

(main image) Longships Lighthouse off Land's End, Cornwall, seen during Storm Desmond in December 2015

(far left x4) Lighthouses come in a variety of shapes, sizes, positions and colours

PIRATES
Ruthless robbers of the seas

DID YOU KNOW?
North African Barbary pirates kidnapped thousands of English people for slavery from the South Coast, up until the 1800s

A galleon typical of ocean-going pirate ships from the 1700s

Thou shalt not steal

Shipping has always been the main way of moving goods long distances. In ancient times, cities and empires that traded on the seas were generally wealthy, but their ships full of valuable goods attracted the attention of thieves. Piracy is the act of raiding another vessel with the intention of stealing what is on board. It started before the times of the Greeks in the Mediterranean Sea, where trade routes were close to the shore, making it easy to hide around headlands on the rocky coasts. Our culture nowadays has a rather romantic view of pirates wearing eye patches and digging for buried treasure. In reality, they were murdering thieves who brought terror to the seas, especially by kidnapping and selling people as slaves. The misery caused by pirates is not just an ancient thing; pirates operate today especially off the coast of Africa, requiring naval forces to protect the waterways.

LEARNING POINT

Do you know what envy is? It is to be discontent with what you have, compared with others. It leads to 'coveting' which is to long to have their stuff for ourselves. It is a sin which leads to other sins such as theft. Our nature is corrupt and we are so ready to envy and covet. Christians though are told to be content, not seeking *earthly* riches, because they already have Jesus Himself who cares for them and makes them rich (Matthew 19:21).

Modern anti-piracy operations by the Indian Navy (right) and Royal Navy (below)

THE BIBLE SAYS . . .
'Let your conversation [conduct] be without covetousness; and be content.' (Hebrews 13:5)

Since publication of the fictional story *Treasure Island* (1883) parrots are often portrayed as sitting on a pirate's shoulder

The pirate's flag of a skull and crossbones, known as the Jolly Roger

DID YOU KNOW?
One of the most infamous pirates in the Caribbean, Edward Teach, known as Blackbeard, was killed by the Royal Navy in 1718

Actors playing the part of pirates at a festival in the Cayman Islands, Caribbean in 2012. A pirate's hat is called a 'tricorne.'

THE SLAVE TRADE

not legally anyway

Trading human lives across the ocean—but not any more*

A slave ship from the port of Liverpool

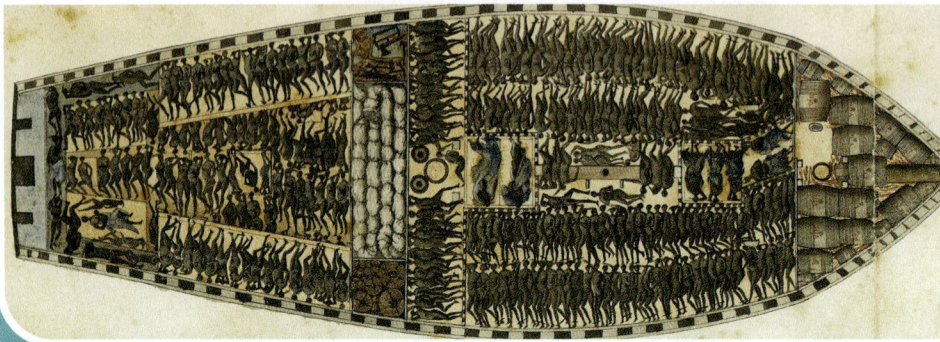

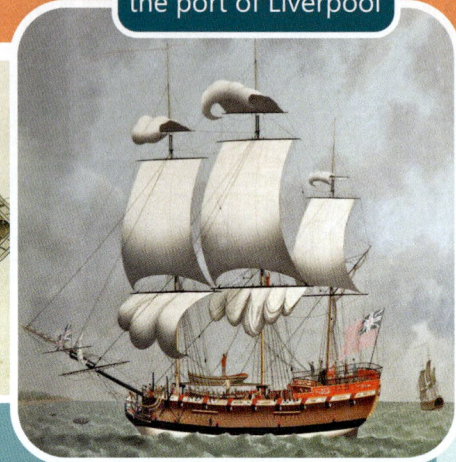

A story of misery ... and of amazing grace

Slavery has sadly been a feature of every empire through history (e.g. see Genesis 37:28). From the 1500s into the 1800s, slavery was big business, as Europeans sold goods to African tribal leaders in exchange for slaves, who were taken across the Atlantic Ocean and sold. Conditions on board the 'slavers' (specially built slave ships, see images above) were horrendous and about 1 in 5 of the slaves and crew died on the voyages. It was a truly inhumane and degrading trade.

Thankfully all that changed from the early 1800s, because the British outlawed slavery and sent the Royal Navy to police the seas, intercepting and stopping slave traders. How did this remarkable change take place? A wicked slave trader called John Newton was convicted of his sin and brought to faith in Jesus Christ. He helped his friend and Member of Parliament William Wilberforce, who, after many years of struggle, managed to bring in anti-slavery laws. It was deeply-held Christian values of love and compassion which made the difference! Christians believe that every person is made in God's image, and is precious. John Newton became a preacher of God's free grace to sinners like himself, and wrote one of the most loved hymns of all time—'Amazing grace!' (see next page).

(far left) A medallion from the Society for the Abolition of the Slave Trade; (left) Over 12 million slaves were taken on these routes

AM I NOT A MAN AND A BROTHER?

North America
Europe
Asia
Atlantic Ocean
India
Africa
Pacific Ocean
South America
Indian Ocean
Atlantic Ocean

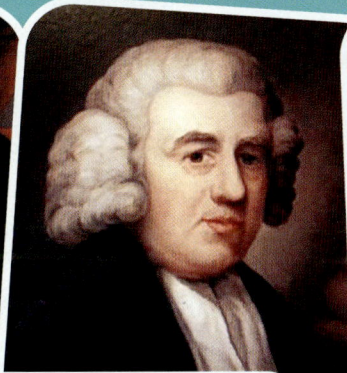

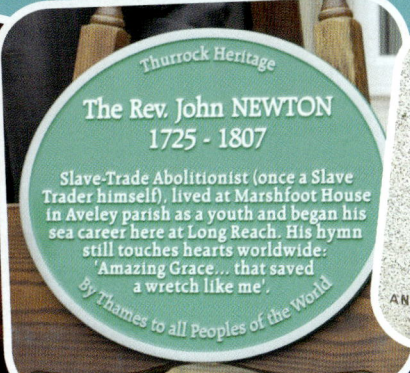

The Rev. John NEWTON
1725 - 1807

Slave-Trade Abolitionist (once a Slave Trader himself), lived at Marshfoot House in Aveley parish as a youth and began his sea career here at Long Reach. His hymn still touches hearts worldwide: 'Amazing Grace... that saved a wretch like me'.

JOHN NEWTON CLERK
ONCE AN INFIDEL AND LIBERTINE
A SERVANT OF SLAVES IN AFRICA WAS
BY THE RICH MERCY OF OUR
LORD AND SAVIOUR JESUS CHRIST
PRESERVED RESTORED PARDONED
AND APPOINTED TO PREACH THE FAITH HE
HAD LONG LABOURED TO DESTROY
NEAR 16 YEARS AS CURATE OF THIS PARISH
AND 28 YEARS AS RECTOR OF St MARY WOOLNOTH

(above left to right) William Wilberforce; John Newton, a plaque near London remembering him, and his grave in Olney

LEARNING POINT

By nature, you and I are slaves. How is that? We may not realise it because we are blinded to the truth (2 Corinthians 4:3-4). We are slaves because of the fear of death (Hebrews 2:14-15), and we also serve our own sinful desires (Titus 3:3). Even when we try and be good before God, it doesn't set us free—we cannot free ourselves, as we cannot keep God's holy law perfectly (Acts 13:39).

But there is wonderful news! Someone has come in great power to free those in slavery who cry unto Him in their need. Who has come? It is the Lord Jesus, God who became Man. The truth which He speaks gives freedom (John 8:32). Have you or I ears to hear this?

THE BIBLE SAYS ...
'The Spirit of the Lord GOD is upon me [Jesus] ... to proclaim liberty to the captives, and the opening of the prison to them that are bound.' (Isaiah 61:1)

A Royal Navy ship capturing the slave ship *El Almirante*, freeing 466 slaves

Amazing grace ! (how sweet the sound)
    That saved a wretch like me !
I once was lost, but now am found,
    Was blind, but now I see.

'Twas grace that taught my heart to fear,
    And grace my fears relieved;
How precious did that grace appear
    The hour I first believed!

Through many dangers, toils, and snares,
    I have already come;
'Tis grace has brought me safe thus far,
    And grace will lead me home.

The Lord has promised good to me,
    His word my hope secures;
He will my shield and portion be
    As long as life endures.

Yes, when this flesh and heart shall fail,
    And mortal life shall cease;
I shall possess, within the veil,
    A life of joy and peace.

The earth shall soon dissolve like snow,
    The sun forbear to shine;
But God, who called me here below,
    Will be forever mine.

MERCY SHIPS

Using ships to take help to those living in poverty

"Let us do good unto all"

Mercy Ships is a Christian international health charity that sends hospital ships to some of the poorest countries in the world, delivering vital, free healthcare to people in desperate need.

On this page: An eye test; amusing a grateful child; and an engineer

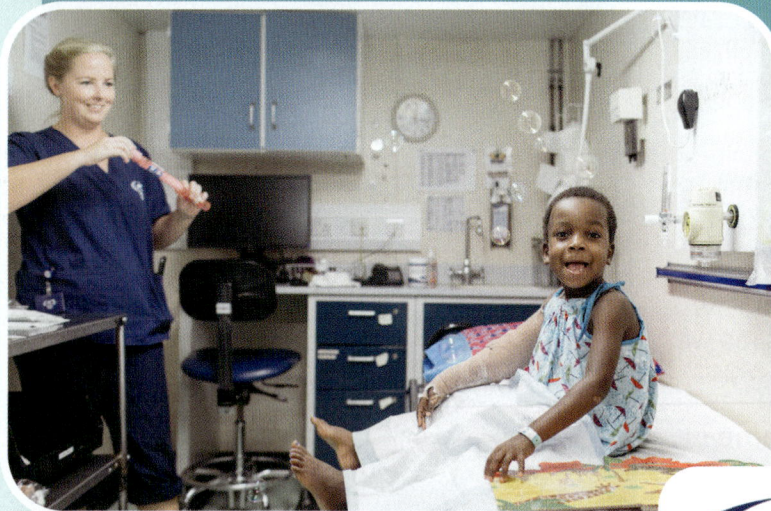

Founded in 1978, Mercy Ships has worked in over 55 countries and provided more than 100,000 free life-changing surgeries. They work closely with African countries so that together, they can make a difference in the long-term.

The charity follows the 2,000-year-old example of Jesus by bringing hope and healing to people who face difficult medical problems. In sub-Saharan Africa, 9 out of 10 people cannot get surgery when they need it. Mercy Ships believes every person is valuable and helps people whoever they are.

It takes a crew to run a hospital ship. Each year, more than 3,000 volunteers from over 60 countries serve on board the charity's two ships. Volunteers not only commit to spending months without pay, but cover their own living expenses. For many, it is an opportunity to serve their Lord and Saviour, and they feel a 'calling' to join the crew. Only half of their volunteers are medics, as they need maritime crew, cooks, electricians, school teachers to educate the volunteers' children, cleaners, and so on.

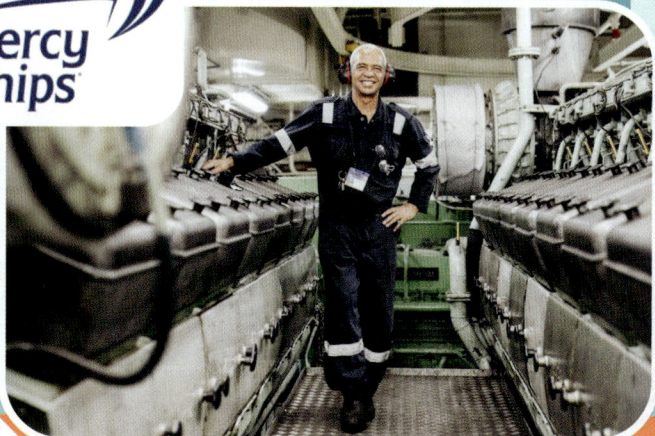

Mercy Ships

Their two ships

The *Global Mercy* (below) has six operating theatres and berths for 600 volunteers; it is the largest charity-run hospital ship in the world. They also have the converted ferry *Africa Mercy* with five operating theatres, berths for 400 volunteers and 80 ward beds.

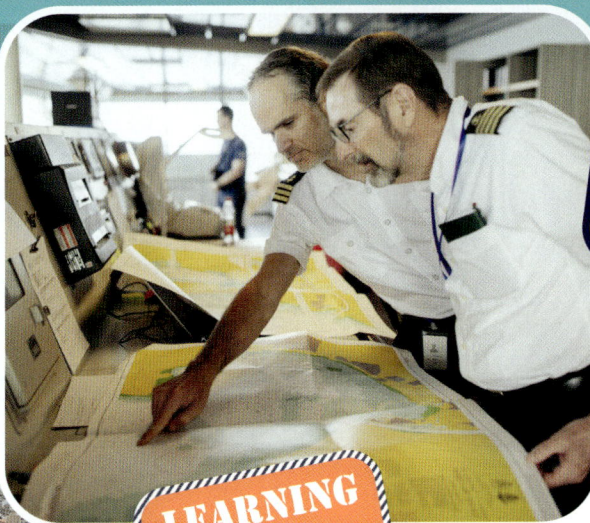

LEARNING POINT

What is mercy? It is when a helpless person is shown compassion and helped out of difficulty; and not because they have earned it or paid for it. As lost sinners, do we *deserve* compassion from God? Romans 3:12 says that there is no-one that does good. How then can we be saved? In Micah 7:18, the prophet declares that there is no-one like God, because **He delights in mercy!** God in His mercy has made a way for all who feel their need: "Believe on the Lord Jesus Christ."

THE BIBLE SAYS . . . 'Not by works of righteousness which we have done, but according to his mercy he saved us.' (Titus 3:5)

The newest vessel in the fleet, the 174m long, 37,000 tonne *Global Mercy*

Mercy Ships' mission:
1. **Provide surgical and medical care**
2. **Train local medical professionals**
3. **Improve health facilities**

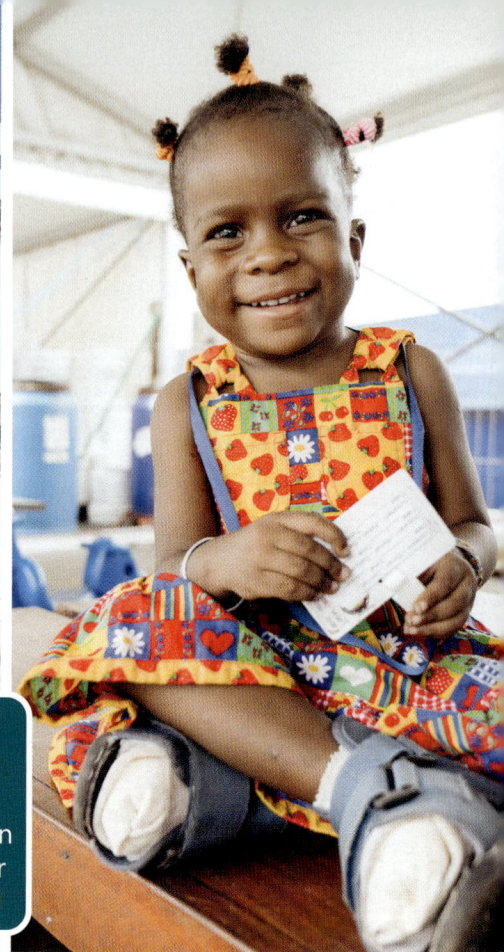

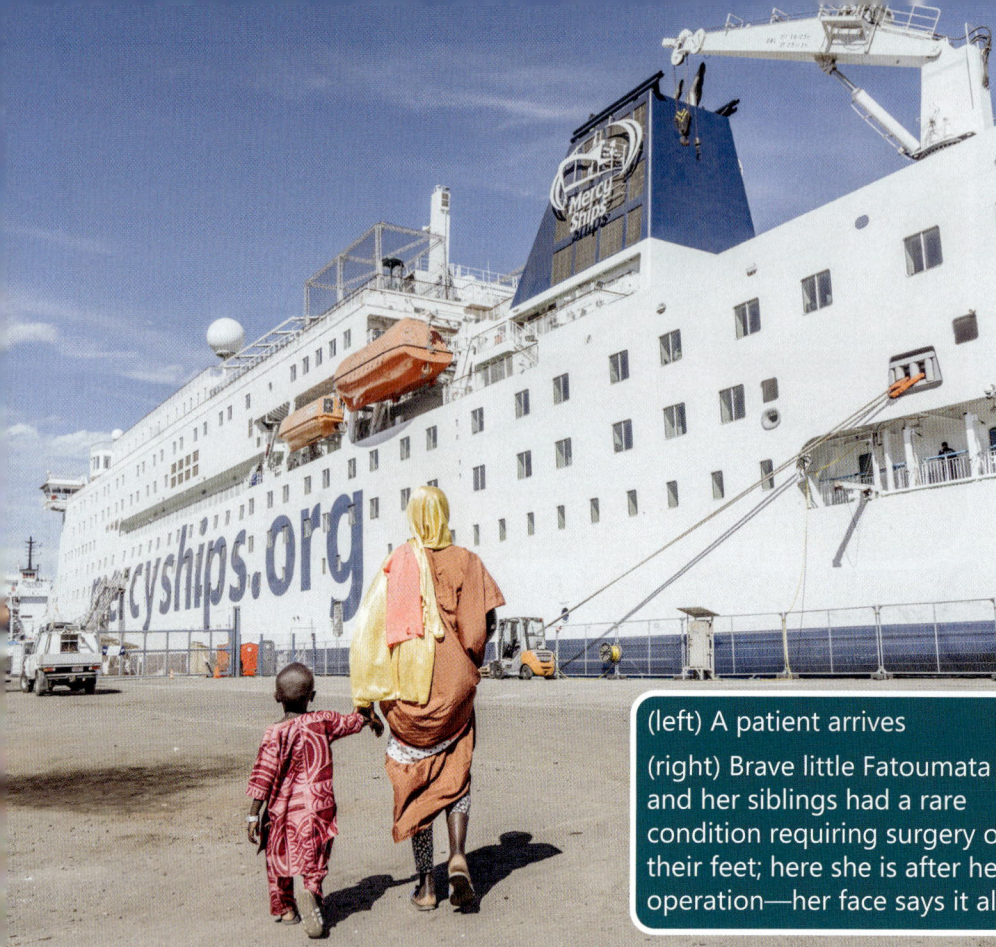

(left) A patient arrives

(right) Brave little Fatoumata and her siblings had a rare condition requiring surgery on their feet; here she is after her operation—her face says it all

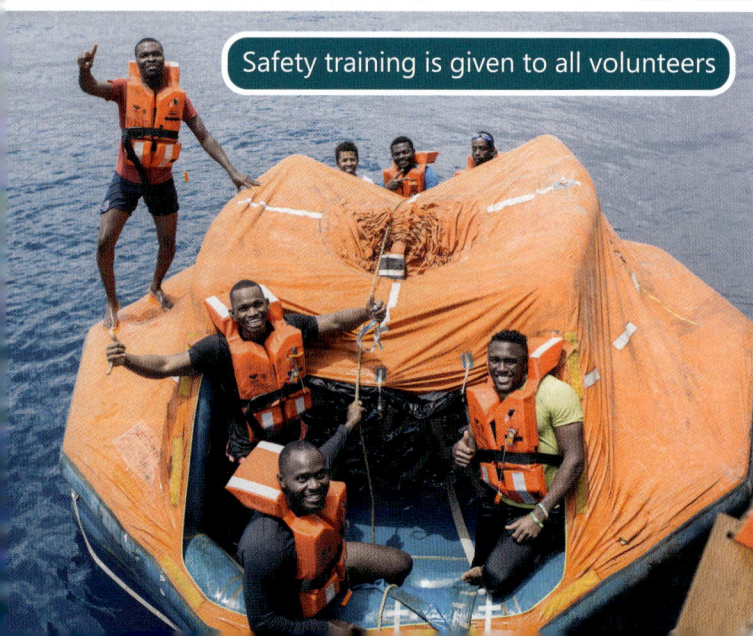

Safety training is given to all volunteers

The *Global Mercy* is nudged into her berth by tugboat on the historic island of Malta, in the Meditteranean Sea, where the Apostle Paul and Luke were shipwrecked (see p44)

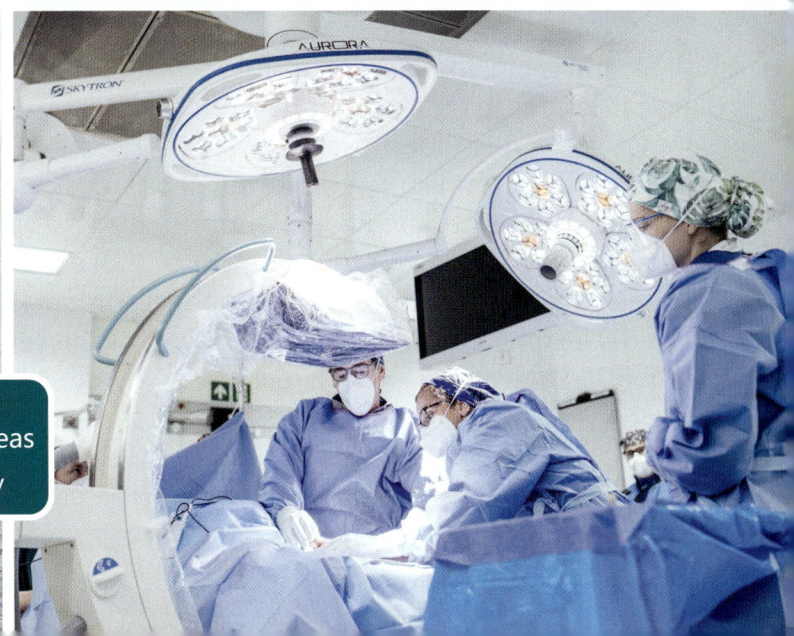

(left) *Global Mercy* and *Africa Mercy* sail together on calm seas

(right) An operation underway

PORTS & HARBOURS
Safe and convenient resting places for seagoing ships and boats

Any port in a storm!

Ships and boats need somewhere to load and offload their cargo and passengers—these places are called **ports** if they have facilities like cranes, storage areas and passenger terminals. Ports are always best if they are protected from rough seas, because large waves would damage or sink the vessel by smashing it against the quayside, and make embarking or disembarking dangerous and difficult. It is usual therefore to locate a port within a **harbour** (or haven), which is any sheltered body of water where ships or boats can be moored, left at anchor, or dock at a quayside. Harbours may be *natural* (such as in bays or river estuaries), or *man-made* (where stone or concrete walls have been built to deflect waves back out into the sea. These walls are known as *breakwaters*.)

Busy ports require deep enough water to accommodate the draught of large ships, so a depth of 10-12 metres is required, and dredging may be needed to maintain it. Some ports have large pens called *basins*, which can be blocked off using gates to hold in the water, so that the low tide does not cause the ships to hit the bottom. They also provide full protection from waves.

Seahouses harbour, Northumberland

LEARNING POINT

If a ship is caught at sea in rough weather, reaching a port or harbour is a welcome relief for those on board. In the terrible storm suffered by Paul and Luke (page 44), the ship's captain had an opportunity to stop at the port of Fair Havens when the weather was getting worse, but he and most of those on board wanted to press on to a better port to spend the winter. How foolish that decision proved to be, and nearly cost them their lives! They under-estimated the frightening power of the sea, and under-valued safety until it was too late.

Life is like a voyage. Many men and women are like those on board that ship. They don't want to be safe in Christ, because they want to carry on, hoping for earthly pleasure, deceiving themselves that the storm of God's wrath won't come, or at least not yet. May that not be you or me.

THE BIBLE SAYS . . .
'Be merciful unto me, O God, be merciful unto me: . . . until these calamities be overpast.' (Psalm 57:1)

Hide me, O my Saviour, hide,
Till the storm of life is past;
Safe into the haven guide;
O receive my soul at last!

Charles Wesley 1707-1788

DID YOU KNOW?
The world's busiest port is Shanghai, China, which in 2020 handled over 43 million 20-foot containers (equivalent)

Three majestic ocean-going liners in the Port of Southampton, before 1931

BEACH HOLIDAY

A break at the coast for some sea air and sandy feet

I do like to be beside the seaside

The English have loved seaside holidays since the 1800s, when the Victorians made 'sea dipping' fashionable—though most people couldn't swim. It was a pasttime for the wealthy, as in those days swimwear was not considered modest, so mobile changing rooms called *bathing machines* were wheeled into the water. Seaside holidays reached their peak in the UK in the 1950s and 1960s due to the *Holidays with Pay Act 1938*. For the first time, working class people could afford to go on holiday every year. Coastal towns like Eastbourne, Hastings, Cromer and Scarborough became even more popular resorts, with hotels, boarding houses and holiday camps. Deck chairs, gift shops, ice cream parlours, fish and chip shops, amusement arcades, crazy golf, bandstands, beach huts and piers were all common around the English coast.

As people have grown wealthier, foreign holidays have become the 'norm', as better weather is almost guaranteed. Many English seaside resorts have become run down, but Devon and Cornwall are still popular.

Then and now: (above) bathing machines in shallow water, Ostend, Belgium, 1913; (below) parasailing over the warm water of the Caribbean Sea, near Cancun, Mexico

LEARNING POINT

How do you feel when your holiday comes to an end? I'm sure some are glad to get home, but for many it is a time of sadness. It is wonderful to have a break from our busy lives, take in the smell of sea air and enjoy an ice cream or two. The saying that "all good things must come to an end" is true, isn't it? However, Christians have Heaven to look forward to; a place of perfect happiness without end; where no-one will ever say that they have had enough, because Jesus is there, the One who is so precious to them!

THE BIBLE SAYS ...
'God shall wipe away all tears from their eyes; and there shall be no more death ... for the former things are passed away.' (Revelation 21: 4)

(top) Buckets, spades and sandcastles at Maenporth Beach near Falmouth, Cornwall

(below left) A beach holiday isn't complete without an ice cream!

(below right) A gift shop overflowing with beach stuff for kids, St Ives harbour, Cornwall

DID YOU KNOW?
Rubbing talcum powder (baby powder) into your feet is a great way to get the sand off them after a day at the beach. Try it!

LIFEGUARDS

Watching swimmers and surfers for safety

Lifeguard training, US military

Ready to spring into action

If you have had a beach holiday, it is likely that you will have seen lifeguards. Their job is to watch the water for anyone who may be in distress and rush to the aid of those at risk of drowning. When an emergency happens, they need to draw on their training which has prepared them to be fit and strong enough, and helps them make life-saving decisions. The job requires patience and diligence, though, as they spend most of the time just watching those in the water.

It is common for lifeguards to put red and yellow flags out on the beach to show where it is safe to swim, and black and white chequered flags for the surfing zone. There are unseen currents, called rips, which can drag swimmers away from the beach, and it is always wise to listen to the lifeguards on duty and follow their instructions. Swimming between the flags also ensures you are never too far from a lifeguard, so they can reach you faster and they are more likely to see if you are in difficulty before you even call for help.

DID YOU KNOW?
Worldwide over 200,000 people die by drowning every year—over 90% are in Africa and Asia

LEARNING POINT

Lifeguards do an amazing job. How thankful we should be if there are lifeguards on duty when we are at the beach. However, they are only human; the sea can be crowded, and large waves can put people out of sight. They simply *cannot* see everyone all the time, especially given that they have to pack up before it gets dark.

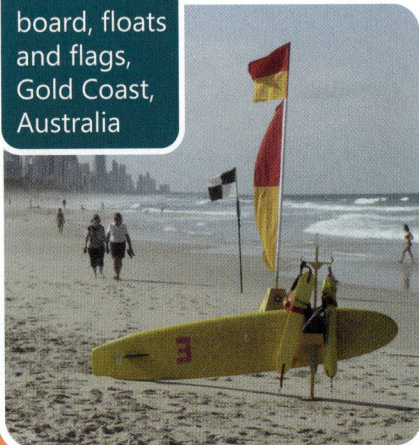
Surf Rescue board, floats and flags, Gold Coast, Australia

But there is One who can always see and hear everything, 24 hours a day, 365 days a year, no matter the location. The LORD God is always ready to hear those who cry unto Him in their need, and save them! Whether it be someone who has felt their sin for the first time and cries for forgiveness, or a mature Christian who is having trouble in their life. Such who feel that they are sinking in the pressures of life can call upon Him who is strong and mighty to save (Isaiah 63:1).

THE BIBLE SAYS . . .
The LORD's hand is not shortened, that it cannot save; neither his ear heavy, that it cannot hear.' (Isaiah 59:1)

(above and top right) Lifeguards can watch from fixed stations or mobile platforms such as this truck

(below) A lifeguard jumps off his watchtower

(right: centre and bottom) A demonstration using a 'waterbike' (personal watercraft) with a rescue sled

GLOSSARY

Out of your depth with some difficult words? Help is here.

Berth: Sleeping place on a ship, or a place in the water where a ship docks.

Buoyancy: The ability of a ship to float caused by the upward force of the water on the ship.

Capsize: When a boat or ship rolls over and turns upside down in the water.

Coxswain: (pronounced 'coxn') Traditional name for a boat captain, still used for all-weather lifeboats.

Cruise ship: Passenger ship designed as a floating hotel which takes holidaymakers from place to place.

Diving bell: A pressurized chamber like a mini-submarine lowered on a steel cable to transport divers.

Dredge: The act of removing mud, sand or silt from the bottom of a river or sea bed. Dredgers work by scooping the material up into the ship and allowing the water to drain away, then taking the material away.

Embark: To board or get on a ship to start a journey. To disembark is to get off after a journey.

Fillet: (verb) To remove the bones from fish, leaving just the flesh (meat) and skin.

Gills: The part of a fish allowing it to breathe underwater (their lungs), often seen as slits behind their eyes.

HMS: His (or Her) Majesty's Ship; title given to warships of the (British) Royal Navy.

Iceberg: Huge chunks of ice which float in the oceans, typically after breaking off from an ice sheet.

Knot: The measurement of a ship or boat's speed. 1 knot = 1 nautical mile per hour. A nautical mile is 1.15 miles and is equivalent to 1 minute of latitude (1/60th of a degree) so is convenient for navigation. The term 'knot' came from the way speed was measured, by throwing some wood into the sea tied to a rope with knots in it. A sailor would count the number of knots which the ship let out in a given time.

Liner: Ocean liners are passenger ships mainly used for transport across seas or oceans.

List / listing: When a ship takes on water or the load moves and then it leans over to one side.

Logbook: (or log) A record of important events happening on a ship, filled out at least daily.

Maiden voyage: The first trip made by a ship once it has entered service.

Marine: Found in or produced by the sea, e.g. animal or plant life, and the environment it is found in.

Maritime: Meaning 'to do with the sea' especially seafaring (sailing / shipping).

Mooring (to moor): A line, anchor or cable which holds a ship in position, or a place made for this.

Morse (code): A type of alphabet where each letter A-Z comprises different combinations of dots and dashes (short or long electrical pulses), which enables messages to be sent by radio or through wires.

Nautical: Similar to 'maritime', meaning something especially related to sailors and navigation.

Naval: To do with a navy. A navy is an armed force comprising ships and other sea-going vessels.

Quay / Quayside: A platform built alongside or over water for loading and unloading ships/boats.

RNLB: Royal National Life Boat, the title preceeding the names of boats in service with the RNLI.

Saline / Salinity: Salty; the measure of how salty water is, i.e. how much salt for a given volume of water.

Sea bed: The floor at the bottom of the sea; the ground below the sea (whether rocky, sandy, etc).

Seasickness: Motion sickness when the constant moving of a ship makes someone vomit or feel sick.

Self-righting: When a boat is designed so that, if it capsizes, it will gradually roll back the right way up.

Snorkel / snorkeling: Diving equipment comprising goggles and a breathing tube which allows a swimmer at the surface to breathe when their face is in the water, useful for watching marine life.

Slave: Someone who is kept captive and forced to work against their will without pay or benefits.

Sonar: Stands for <u>SO</u>und <u>N</u>avigation <u>A</u>nd <u>R</u>anging; a loud ping is sent out which may bounce off an object and return a signal. The objects distance can be calculated by measuring the time taken.

SOS: International distress code which is *dot dot dot* (S), *dash dash dash* (O), *dot dot dot* (S) in Morse.

S.S.: The title of a ship which normally stands for 'Steam Ship', i.e. powered by steam engine(s).

Trawler: A common type of fishing vessel which works by dragging one or more nets through the water.

Vessel: Ship with lifesaving & navigation equipment, e.g. liner, cruise ship, cargo ship, trawlers, warships etc.

Bible challenge

There is a lot in the Bible about the sea. Can you match up these verses with the right pictures below? One of them might catch you out as I have quoted the word out of context... Answers: page 77

1. Jonah 1:17
2. James 1:6
3. Ezekiel 27:6
4. Genesis 32:12
5. Psalm 107:30
6. Revelation 6:1
7. Acts 27:29
8. 1 Timothy 1:19
9. Numbers 24:24
10. Matthew 4:18

DayOne

Published by: Day One Publications, Ryelands Rd, Leominster, HR6 8NZ
sales@dayone.co.uk
www.dayone.co.uk

Answers to questions on page 75:

1. Jonah 1:17 = J (great/huge fish)
2. James 1:6 = A (wave)
3. Ezekiel 27:6 = G (oar)
4. Genesis 32:12 = K (sand)
5. Psalm 107:30 = H (haven, port)
6. Revelation 6:1 = D (seal - the tricky one!)
7. Acts 27:29 = C (anchor)
8. 1 Timothy 1:19 = B (shipwreck)
9. Numbers 24:24 = F (ship)
10. Matthew 4:18 = E (net)

(left) This photo captures something of the power of the sea. Large waves like this are the remnant of ocean storms. The energy from the wind remains in the water and can travel long distances. Before coming to shore and breaking, these waves are known as 'swell'.

Copyright © Mark Philpott 2023
ISBN 978-1-84625-750-6

Bible quotes are from the Authorised (King James) Version. If words have been replaced for clarity, these are shown in *italics*. If words have been inserted, these are shown in square brackets [ ].

👍 ACKNOWLEDGEMENTS

Recognising help given and the sources of the images in this book

Key: p=page number pp=pages T=top B=bottom L=left R=right C=centre

Mercy Ships https://www.mercyships.org.uk https://www.mercyships.org (USA)
Thanks for assisting with the section of the same name and supply of all photographs on **pp64-67** © Mercy Ships.

Karsten Petersen https://www.global-mariner.dk
Thanks for permission to reproduce the photos of *M/T Stolt Surf* and include excerpts from his eye witness accounts recorded on his website. All images on **pp40-41** are © Karsten Petersen.

The Venerable Robert Townsend / Church In Wales https://www.churchinwales.org.uk
Thanks to the Church in Wales for permission to use an article on Robert from December 2020. Gratitude to Robert for bringing the story up-to-date as included on **pp54-55** and being willing to feature in this book. Image credits: **p54TL** Church in Wales, **p55TL** Robert Townsend.

Ark Encounter https://arkencounter.com
Thanks to Melany Ethridge for supplying the photos on **pp32-33** by permission of Ark Encounter.

Oil and Gas Rigs, p16: reference https://energynow.com/2022/09/the-irrefutable-case-for-a-fossil-future/
For further reading see 'Fossil Future: Why Global Human Florishing Requires More Oil... - Not Less' by Alex Epstein.

Licensed by Creative Commons www.creativecommons.org/licenses + www.flickr.com
License details available at above web address. Unless noted in square brackets after each attribution, image license will be 'CC BY 2.0'; abbreviations are used where the license type differs: SA='CC BY-SA 2.0'; ND='CC BY-ND 2.0'; 3='CC BY-3.0', etc. All photos have been sourced from **flickr.com**, except those suffixed '[W]' which are sourced from **https://commons.wikimedia.org/**.

Front cover, p3, p47 "Whitestarline.svg" by Whistlerpro [SA3,W]; **p1** "Guadalupe Island Great White Shark Cage Diving.jpg" by Sharkcrew [SA4,W]; **p11TL** "JMSDF Sōryū class submarines-02.png" by Ministry of Defense Japan [4,W]; **TR** "Salt" by Marco Zanferrari [SA]; **CR** "Dead Sea 1 070" by Bob McCaffrey [SA]; **B** "Carlsbad Desalination Plant" by vanderhe1 [ND]; **p12** "Surf's Up" by PapaPiper [ND]; **p13T** "St Ives Panorama" by Paul Tomlin; **C** "St, Ives at low tide. Panorama. D3100. DSC_0296-0300." by Robert Pittman [ND]; **BL&BR** "Catch A Wave" & "Broken Reflection" by Andrew; **p15T** "Five masted fully rigged tall ship - Royal Clipper" by Cbuske46 [SA4,W]; **C** "Ocean gyres currents blank.png" by Ingwik [SA3]; **B** "Ulsan Express" by Henry Burrows [SA]; **p17CL** "Rig for repair Invergordon Base Little & Large" by murdoch sutherland [SA,W]; **p19T** "Fischkutter vor Ameland.jpg" by Hartmut Schmidt Heidelberg [SA4,W]; **BL** "aboard trawler African Queen" by Zatoka33 [SA4,W]; **BR** "Royal Greenland trawler" by EHRENBERG Kommunikation [SA,W]; **p20TL** "Resting - Grundarfjörður, Iceland" by Ron Kroetz [ND]; **CL** "Faroese trawler in action, Faroe Islands" by Erik Christensen [SA4,W]; **BL** "Fishing trawlers" by Joseph Novak; **p20R-21** "Greenland fishing trawler BINGO III - GR 2-122– MMSI 331214000" by Gordon Leggett [SA4,W]; **p22T** "Yu Diving October 2010" by Yu Diving [SA]; **B** "INTRO DIVE_Dolphin Reef Eilat - Tony Malkevist" by Photo Gallery Israeli Ministry of Tourism [ND]; **p24T** "Carcharodon megalodon fossil shark jaw (reconstruction) (late Cenozoic) 2" by James St. John; **B** "Hammerhead Shark" by Marko Dimitrijevic [SA]; **p25T** "Great White Shark (Carcharodon carcharias) attacking a fish lure" by Bernard DUPONT [SA]; **BL&BR** "Great White Shark" by Elias Levy (x2); **p26** "Colossal Squid A.jpg" by Benjamindancer [SA3,W]; **p27** x3 by NOAA Ocean Exploration: **T** "Jelly" [SA]; **CL** "Expedition to the Deep Slope 2006: May 31 Log" [SA]; **B** "Ctenophore" [SA]; **p29TR** "Augustasaurus BW.jpg" by Nobu Tamura [3]; **C** "Paleo Hall at HMNS" by Kim Alaniz; **CL** "Icelandic Sea Monster Museum" by Jennifer Boyer [ND]; **p30BL** "Kronosaurus queenslandicus" by Nobu Tamura [3]; **p31TR** "mosasaur - Cleveland Museum of Natural History" by Tim Evanson [SA]; **p34T** "RHL Augsburg (IMO 9378022).jpg" (flipped) by Niels Johannes [SA4]; **pp34-35** "Querschnitt eines SCOT 8000-Tankers" by Wappen-Reederei GmbH & Co. KG [SA2 DE,W]; **p35T** "MetacentricHeight.svg" by Life of Riley [SA2.5,W]; **p36CL** "Anchor" by Greg Clarke [ND]; **p37BL** "Capitan officers paint the starboard anchor gold   commemorating" by Official U.S. Navy Page; **p39T&BR**

"ship1175"&"ship0726" by NOAA Photo Library; **p43T** "Shipwreck of MV Alta" by Colm Ryan [SA4,W]; **CL** "Collision of Costa Concordia 24.jpg" by Rvongher [SA3,W]; **BR** "expl4133" by NOAA Photo Library; **p44C** "Ancora-cireco-2019.jpg" by Massimo D'Alessandro [SA4,W]; **B** "Il-ponta tal Munxar.jpg" by AntonellaVella [SA4,W]; **p46** "Massive iceberg" by David Stanley; **p48** "RMS St Helena London (16358540002).jpg" by David Stanley [W]; **p49TL&inset** "Put Away Your Toys"&"Four Men In a Boat" by A Guy Named Nyal [SA]; **TR** "The Lifeboat" by Harley Flowers [SA]; **CL** "USS HARPERS FERRY (LSD 49)....jpg" by US Naval Forces Central Command; **CR** "Katie's feet" by Simon P [ND]; **BL** "Life Raft Training..." by U.S. Army Corps of Engineers; **BR** "Life raft" by Matthew Robinson; **p51TR** "Royal Navy Image 45155248.jpg" by Defence Imagery [SA]; **pp52-53L** "Coast Guard 47' Motor Lifeboat in Morro Bay, CA..." by Mike Baird; **p54CR** "Looe Festival by the Sea" by Gerry Wood [ND]; **p56C** "Torre de Hércules, La Coruña, España...jpg" by Diego Delso [SA1]; **p57 main image** "Beachy Head Lighthouse 8th October 2013" by Rob Wassell [ND]; **TR** "Omaezaki Lighthouse lens.jpg" by Qurren; **BR** "Currituck Beach Light - stairs.jpg" by rpertiet [W]; **p58TL** "lighthouse" by scott1346; **CLT** "Makapu'u Lighthouse" by Jon Parise [SA]; **CLB** "Cape Hatteras Lighthouse at sunset" by John Buie; **BL** "Smeaton's Tower on Plymouth Hoe in Devon, UK" by Herbythyme; **p60TR** "Pirates !" by Rene Menson; **p61TR** "Jolly Roger" by J. Hutsch [W]; **p62BC** "Map of both intercontinental and transatlantic slave trade in Africa" by KuroNekoNiyah [SA4,W]; **p63CR** "John newton plaque.jpg" by Susan Yates [SA3,W]; **p69T** "Stormy Newhaven Harbour" by Mark; **p70B** "Parasailing over the Water of the Riviera Maya" by Grand Velas Riviera Maya [SA]; **p71T** "Buckets, Spades And Sandcastle" by Henry Burrows [SA]; **p73TL** "Baywatch" by Kyle Monahan; **p73CR&BR** "RNLI Lifeguard demonstration" by Dan Marsh; **BL** "IMG_8023" by David; **p79** "The Three Queens" by Andrew; **Back cover TR** "Great white shark (Carcharodon carcharias)" by Elias Levy; **BL** "Purple short leg cast.JPG" by Pagemaker787 [SA4].

Open Government License, UK (OGL) / Government Open Data License - India (GODL)

These images are reproduced under the OGL, http://www.nationalarchives.gov.uk/doc/open-government-license/version/1/ and are © Crown Copyright [year]: **p18** Photo: Royal Navy/MOD [2013]; **p53R** LA(Phot) Dave Sterratt [2012]; **p80** POA(Phot) Paul A'Barrow [2012]. This image is reproduced under the GODL, https://data.gov.in/sites/default/files/Gazette_Notification_OGDL.pdf: **p60C** Indian Navy. All the above have been sourced from **https://commons.wikimedia.org/**.

Icons from the Noun Project https://thenounproject.com (items marked '~' also appear on **p7**)

Cover, p3, p36~ Anchor by Joep van der Linden; **p4** Ship Wheel by hind andaloussi; **p10~** drink straw by Martin, ~ ban by Alexander; **p12~** tide by Gregor Cresnar; **p14~** Loop by Mustofa Bayu; **p16~** Flame by Mourad Mokrane; **p18~** Fish by Laymik; **p22~** bubbles by IronSV; **p24~** Shark by Gilberto; **p24** Heat by Isma Ruiz; aerodynamic by glyph.faisalovers; Shark (teeth) by Dmitry Vasiliev; smell by Chintuza; **p26~** Arrow by Alice Design; **p28~** Mosaurus by Raf Verbraeken; ~ waves (part) by Loritas Medina; **p32~** Umbrella by Vectors Market; **p34~** Fan by Studio Het Mes; **p34** bath toy by SUPRIYANTO YANTO; rudder by Toni Bordoy; warning triangle by Kmg Design; Sofa by Berkah; beam by Bakunetsu Kaito; Shield by HideMaru; **p38~** storm by J703; **p42~** sinking boat by Luis Prado; **p44** Boat by Pedro Santos; **p46~** titanic by Pawel Rak; **p50~** SOS Emergency by Hali Gali Harun; **p54** Microphone by metami septiana; **p56~** Lighthouse by Nociconist; **p60~** jolly roger by parkjisun; **p62~** chains by Cédric Villain; **p64~** helpful by Adrien Coquet; **p68~** Parking by Rahma; **p70~** Travel by Creative Stall; **p72~** help by Iconographer.

Shutterstock Stock images available from https://www.shutterstock.com

Front cover T: silvergull; B: Jag_cz; **pp2-3** Alvov; **p6** Jellyman Photography; **p17** TL AzmanMD; **p23** Subphoto.com; **pp30-31** main image Daniel Eskridge; **pp58-59** main image Mick Blakey; **p61** main image Blue Sky imagery.

Permission granted to reproduce copyright material in this book is gratefully acknowledged. If there are errors or omissions, we apologise. Please contact us so that this can be incorporated in future reprints or editions.

A Royal Navy Sea King search and rescue helicopter lowers a winchman to an RNLI 'D Class' inshore lifeboat to practice for transferring an injured person

Other books in the series include:

Farm School

Driving School

Flight School

Contact Day One for more details

More titles being added to the series